P9-BZZ-720

SCRIBES, WARRIORS
AND KINGS

NEW ASPECTS OF ANTIQUITY

General Editor: COLIN RENFREW

Consulting Editor for the Americas: JEREMY A. SABLOFF

WILLIAM L. FASH

SCRIBES, WARRIORS AND KINGS

The City of Copán and the Ancient Maya

Drawings by Barbara W. Fash

with 120 illustrations, 11 in color

Thames and Hudson

For Gordon R. Willey

Frontispiece: Detail from an incised peccary skull found in Tomb 1 showing two figures beside an altar, with a stela in the background. Compare ill. 24.

Any copy of this book issued by the publisher as a paperback is sold subject to the condition that it shall not, by way of trade or otherwise, be lent, resold, hired out or otherwise circulated without the publisher's prior consent in any form of binding or cover other than that in which it is published, and without a similar condition including these words being imposed on a subsequent purchaser.

© 1991 Thames and Hudson Ltd, London

First published in the USA in 1991 by Thames and Hudson Inc., 500 Fifth Avenue, New York, New York 10110.

Library of Congress Catalog Card Number 91-65316

All Rights Reserved. No part of this publication may be reproduced or transmitted in any form or by any means, electronic or mechanical, including photocopy, recording or any other information storage and retrieval system, without permission in writing from the publisher.

Printed and bound in Singapore by CS Graphics Pte Ltd

CONTENTS

FOREWORD FROM THE EDITORS

Scholarly understanding of ancient Maya civilization is increasing at a very rapid pace. New insights into the development and workings of this fascinating culture appear frequently, with no indication that they are about to abate. In the past two decades alone, traditional views on the growth of the Maya in the lowlands of southern Mesoamerica have undergone such major revision that current perspectives often bear little resemblance to those held just a few years ago. Amidst all the intellectual excitement and burgeoning enlightenment about the Maya, however, there are some looming clouds that threaten to impede progress in Maya studies. One of the most ominous of these clouds is the growing split between scholars who focus on the ancient Maya élite, and those studying the non-élite peasants, merchants, and craftspeople. The former, stimulated by the remarkable strides made recently in the decipherment of Maya hieroglyphic writing, have made significant progress in elucidating the nature of Maya rulership, particularly during the Classic Period (AD 250–900). The latter, encouraged by the growing scope and sophistication of studies of ancient Maya settlement over the lowland landscape, have gained important new insights into the functioning of Maya cities and the agricultural systems that supported them. These two broad areas of research ought to be complementary, but are all too often separated by an intellectual chasm.

Fortunately, ongoing research at the great Maya city of Copán, in the Central American country of Honduras, is starting to bridge the yawning gap between élite and non-élite studies. This beautiful site, renowned for its striking sculpture and architecture, has been the focus of scholarly attention for many decades, and the history of archaeological fieldwork at the site mirrors the general changes that Maya studies have undergone over the past century. Copán was first brought to public attention 150 years ago by the writings and drawings of John Stephens and Frederick Catherwood, and later in the 19th century by Alfred Maudslay. The first scientific excavations in the Maya lowlands were initiated at Copán 100 years ago by the Peabody Museum of Harvard University. This work was followed by research – as well as restoration – at the site by the Carnegie Institution of Washington, including Sylvanus Morley's pioneering study of the hieroglyphic inscriptions.

Most recently, fieldwork in both urban Copán and the rural area in the surrounding valley has been undertaken by a host of well-known scholars under the overall direction of Gordan Willey, Claude Baudez, William Sanders, and most recently by William Fash, the author of this volume. This new research, which extends from the heart of Copán's ceremonial core, where Fash and his colleagues are currently working, to peasant houses many kilometers from the city center, is helping to refine current views on the entire spectrum of Classic Maya culture, from the lords who ruled Copán to the peasants who labored for them.

In the lucid text that follows, Professor Fash synthesizes the findings of the recent research at Copán, particularly emphasizing the results of the Copán Mosaics Project which he has directed. He perceptively shows how fresh information garnered from breakthroughs in the decipherment of Copán inscriptions, studies of Copán architecture, and excavations in some of the élite buildings can be placed in the context of new understandings of the overall Copán Valley environment and settlement, to produce a richer and fuller picture of the development and ultimate demise of the great city than has hitherto been possible. This new vision of Copán and, by extension, of the Classic Maya world can be glimpsed in the pages below.

Jeremy A. Sabloff

Colin Renfrew

CHAPTER ONE

COPÁN AND CLASSIC MAYA CIVILIZATION

Architecture, sculpture, and painting, all the arts which embellish life, had flourished in this overgrown forest; orators, warriors, and statesmen, beauty, ambition, and glory, had lived and passed away, and none knew that such things had been, or could tell of their past existence . . . It lay before us like a shattered bark in the midst of the ocean, her masts gone, her name effaced, her crew perished, and none to tell whence she came, to whom she belonged, how long on her voyage, or what caused her destruction . . . All was mystery; dark, impenetrable mystery.[1]

The mystery of the Maya

So wrote the American explorer and diplomat John Lloyd Stephens upon his arrival at the Maya ruins of Copán in 1839. Scattered mentions of these and other imposing monuments of the Classic period (AD 250–900) of Maya civilization had made their way into the Spanish colonial archives. But it was not until the publication of Stephens' book, *Incidents of Travel in Central America* (1841), with its glorious illustrations by the English artist Frederick Catherwood, that the world at large had the opportunity to ponder the achievements of this creative and energetic people, and to speculate on the reasons for the demise of its once imposing centers of the arts. Shrouded in jungle, obscured by the passage of centuries and the migration of the original inhabitants from much of the region, the Classic Maya ruins posed a formidable mystery indeed.

Beyond the obvious question of what caused the collapse of the Classic Maya city-states, a whole series of other problems confronted the Western scholars who took up the challenge of reconstructing the history of this lost civilization. Where did it come from? How long did it flourish? What was the nature of the society that gave birth to such breathtaking monuments of art and architecture? And what did the ancient writings record, what matters of state or religion were embedded there?

It was this last question which most fueled the imagination of 19th-century scholars, who set about trying to decipher the Maya hieroglyphic script. Their task was made easier by the publication of the three then-known Maya bark-paper books (the Dresden, Madrid, and Paris codices) by the French abbé Brasseur de Bourbourg, and of the massive compendium of Maya stone monuments produced by Alfred Maudslay for the *Biologia Centrali-Americana* (1889–1902). Maudslay's work spurred the Peabody Museum of

Harvard University to begin reconnaissance work in the Maya area, with a number of volumes published in their *Memoirs* series, beginning in the 1890s. These books enabled scholars to work more concertedly on the inscriptions, and at the same time encouraged other archaeologists to begin different kinds of investigations. The long-term result has been that the ancient Maya are among the most thoroughly scrutinized cultures of the aboriginal New World, the subject of dozens of excavation programs, hundreds of site surveys, countless porings over colonial-period manuscripts, and volumes and volumes of books.

Ironically, today's scholars have come to realize the wisdom of many of Stephens' original interpretations. Stephens correctly surmised that Copán and the other Maya ruins were the remains of indigenous New World peoples, that the human portraits on the monuments represented 'deified kings and heroes'. He also correctly guessed that the writing system recorded the history of the kings and their cities. However, many of Stephens' contemporaries and successors, caught up in the romanticism of the era, proposed far less reasonable reconstructions. The Classic Maya ruins were variously ascribed to the Ten Lost Tribes of Israel, to the Egyptians, to the Phoenicians, to the Javanese, or to the Chinese. Furthermore, early decipherments of the calendrical and astronomical portions of the surviving Maya hieroglyphic texts led researchers to conclude that the written records were concerned primarily with the passage of time and the movement of the heavenly bodies.

As the 20th century advanced, the view became widespread that the main function of Classic Maya writing was to provide astronomical calculations, and to mark the passage of time. This in turn, it was thought, allowed the priests to make astrological considerations of the relative influences of the gods who were patrons of the celestial bodies, days, months, and even numbers, recorded in the Maya texts. By extension, the individuals portrayed on the stone monuments must be either the gods themselves, or the astronomer-priests who were charged with measuring the passage of time and prophesying the future based on auguries of the multitude of supernatural forces which reigned over the days of the year. The Classic Maya, according to conventional wisdom, was a theocratic society, run by benevolent priests who exhorted the ingenuous, peaceful peasant farmers scattered in the countryside to build more temples at their 'vacant ceremonial centers', in honor of the high gods in their pantheon.

Mystery compounded mystery for decades, and it has only been in the past 30 years that scholars have come to recognize the truth of Stephens' assertions, and to re-evaluate their romantic and utopian views of Maya society in the Classic period. Thanks to some brilliant hieroglyphic decipherments beginning in the late 1950s and continuing to this day, and to a more thorough, scientific, and theoretically sophisticated approach to the archaeological investigation of Maya ruins, the Maya have finally emerged from the stilted and idealized vision which 19th- and early 20th-century Western scholars

1 Frederick Catherwood's drawing of the toppled and battered Stela C.

2 Frederick Catherwood's drawing of Stela N, portraying one of Copán's 'deified kings and heroes'.

3 Alfred P. Maudslay, seated at the base of Stela A in 1885.

thrust upon them. It is now understood that the Classic Maya had many of the same problems as other early pre-industrial civilizations: social distinctions leading to the exploitation of the people comprising the lower ranks of society; a trend toward nucleation of population around central places (the 'ceremonial center' of the older model), resulting in crowded and unsanitary conditions and the proliferation of communicable diseases; the aggrandizement of the ruling élite in public buildings and inscribed 'official' history; and intense competition – including warfare – between rival kingdoms, and even between competing high-status lineages within those societies. The humanizing of the Classic Maya, in fact, makes it possible for scholars to compare them more easily and fruitfully with other societies around the world at a similar level of technological and socio-political organization.

Mesoamerica and the Maya

The ancient Maya were but one of many different complex cultures and civilizations which thrived in the culture area referred to as Mesoamerica. This culture area was defined by the anthropologist Paul Kirchoff, who observed that at the time of the Spanish conquest a series of distinctive cultural adaptations were shared among the peoples inhabiting the geographic area comprising all of central and southern Mexico, Guatemala, Belize, El Salvador, and the western half of Honduras, the southern fringe of Nicaragua, and the Nicoya Peninsula of Costa Rica. These shared adaptations included pyramidal platforms supporting masonry structures, the playing of a rubber ballgame in specially-prepared courts, the use of a calendrical system which combined a solar calendar of 365 days with a ritual calendar of 260 days, the use of bark-paper books for recording native history and religious tracts, a pantheon of shared deities (with allowances for regional variation), a dependence on an agricultural system centered around the cultivation of maize, beans, and squash, and numerous other traits.

Among the peoples of ancient Mesoamerica, the Maya were distinguished by a series of cultural adaptations that were appealing to Western scholars who had studied the Classical civilizations of the Mediterranean world. The extensive hieroglyphic texts inscribed on free-standing monoliths, which came to be known as 'stelae' (singular, 'stela'), and their accompanying altars contained records of the passage of time in a number of different calendars. There were ritual calendars of 260 and 819 days; a solar calendar of 365 days; a lunar series recording the lunar month, the day in the lunation and the length of the lunation; a Venus calendar for predicting the appearance and disappearance of that planet as Morning and Evening Star; and a sequential time-reckoning system based on the passage of 360-day cycles, known as the Long Count. Inscriptions were also found on various parts of impressive masonry buildings, often embellished with elaborate pictorial art in stucco or stone and a corbel or 'false' arch in the interior of many structures. Classic Maya art

4 Map of Mesoamerica and its regions, showing some of the most important sites including those mentioned in the text.

focused on gracefully depicted human figures surrounded by a plethora of exotic religious symbols.

Examples of Maya art were recovered in a wide variety of media, including monolithic and architectural monuments, elaborately painted or modeled and carved ceramics, wood, incised bone, chipped stone, and other materials. Because of these advances in the arts and sciences, the perception grew that the Maya were somehow 'special', or more civilized, than the rest of the aboriginal cultures of the New World; they were the Greeks, and the Aztecs were the Romans, so the saying went. As a result, the ancient Maya became the focus of a great deal of research by Western scholars after their 'rediscovery' by Stephens and Catherwood.

At the time of the Spanish conquest in the early 16th century, Maya speakers inhabited about one-third of the land surface of Mesoamerica, stretching from the Isthmus of Tehuantepec on the west to the western sections of Honduras and El Salvador on the east. Within this large area there was tremendous diversity, both geographical and cultural. Geographically, ancient Maya lands

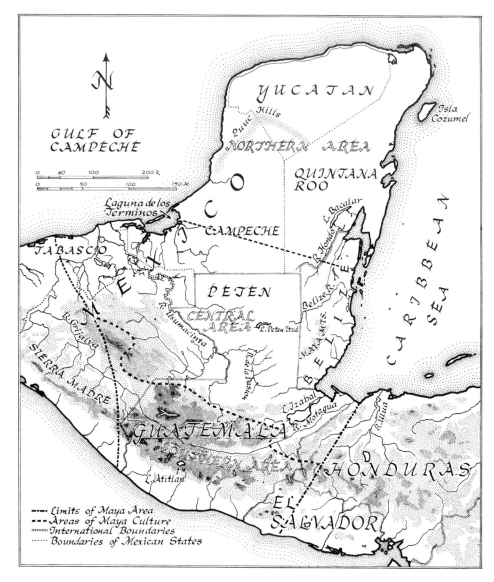

5 Map of the Maya region, showing its three principal areas.

range from humid tropical mangroves in the south, to a lush foothills zone, which in turn gives way to the cool, steep slopes of the highlands of Chiapas, Guatemala, and far western El Salvador. Farther north, the highlands give way to the immense, flat expanse referred to as the Maya lowlands, the hearth of the most dramatic cultural florescence of the so-called Classic period. The lowlands are themselves divided into southern lowlands (northern Guatemala, Belize, and adjacent parts of the Mexican state of Chiapas – characterized by full-fledged tropical rainforests and average annual rainfall of 200–300 cm), and northern lowlands (comprising the Mexican states of Campeche, Yucatán, and Quintana Roo – characterized for the most part by scrub-brush vegetation, thin soils, little surface water, and a mean annual precipitation of less than 200 cm).

Linguistically there were 31 recorded Mayan languages at the time of the Spanish conquest, two of which are now extinct. Speakers of the other languages still occupy different parts of the Maya area. The languages recorded on the hieroglyphic texts of the Classic period include Chol (in the southern lowlands) and Yucatec (in the northern lowlands), and speakers of these two languages still outnumber those of the other Mayan tongues. Culturally the archaeological remains attest to considerable diversity in Precolumbian times as well. Still, there was unquestionably a great wealth of beliefs and customs which were held in common. Much of what we view as physically different should perhaps best be seen simply as different regional manifestations of a common cultural tradition.

Archaeological periods

Archaeologists deal with material remains and, like their colleagues in the natural sciences, classify their evidence in various ways. Just as there are several more or less well-defined cultural zones within the Maya area, so there are three major cultural periods, divided into sub-periods, and further broken down at each site into numerous ceramic phases, which are further divided into complexes, groups, wares, types, varieties, and more. For present purposes, it is well to note the various zones (see illus. 5), and to lay out the chronology of the various periods.

The *Preclassic* period is generally defined as running from 2000 BC to AD 250, subdivided into the Early (2000–1000 BC), Middle (1000–300 BC), and Late (300 BC–AD 250, including a 'Protoclassic' dated AD 100–250).

The *Classic* period is defined as the period during which the lowland Maya carved hieroglyphic inscriptions on stone monuments using the linear system of time-reckoning known as the 'Long Count'. Traditionally, the Classic period has been divided into the Early Classic (AD 250–600) and the Late Classic (AD 600–900). Recently, some scholars have recognized a time of marked interaction with or influence from the great central Mexican metropolis of Teotihuacan at several prominent sites between AD 400 and 700. In order to evaluate these developments across the Maya landscape the term 'Middle Classic' is used. At Copán, the Middle Classic concept is useful for discussing ceramic ties and dating.

The *Postclassic* period runs from AD 900 (the time of the so-called 'collapse' of the Classic period centers in the southern lowlands) to the arrival of the Spanish conquistadores in AD 1519. This period is also divided into an Early Postclassic period (AD 900–1200) and a Late Postclassic period (AD 1200–1519).

TIME	PERIODS	COPAN	CHALCHUAPA	LOS NARANJOS	TIKAL	KAMINALJUYU	
1200	Postclassic	EJAR	Matzin	Rio Blanco		Ayampuc	
1000							
800	Late Classic	CONER	Payu	Yojoa	Eznab	Pamplona	
					Imix		
600	Middle Classic	ACBI	Xocco		Ik	Amatle 2	
					Manik	1	Esper-anza
400	Early Classic	BIJAC	Vec	Eden 2		Aurora	
200	Protoclassic		Late Caynac		Cimi	Arenal	
AD BC	Late Preclassic	CHABIJ	Early Caynac		Cauac	Verbena	
200			Chul	Eden 1	Chuen	Providencia	
400		UIR			Tzec		
600	Middle Preclassic		Kal	Jaral	Eb		
800		Gordon	Colos				
1000		RAYO	Tok				
1200	Early Preclassic						

6 *The major chronological divisions of Maya history, together with the phases for five sites: Copán, Chalchuapa, Los Naranjos, Tikal and Kaminaljuyu.*

Copán as a Classic Maya center

Sylvanus Morley, archaeologist, epigrapher, and dean of Maya archaeology during one of its most productive epochs, lavished some of his highest praise on Copán. In his words, 'Copán may be aptly called "the Athens of the New World", a title the writer has been wont to bestow upon her in drawing analogies from the ancient cities of the Old World; . . . it may be claimed with perfect assurance that no other city of aboriginal America ever attained so high a level of cultural achievement'.[2]

I *The Copán Acropolis seen from the air. The banks of the river are lined by trees, and today the fertile bottomlands and most of the foothills are being used for agriculture once more.*

7 *View to the north over Ballcourt A-III as envisioned by Tatiana Proskouriakoff in the 1930s. The Great Plaza is visible in the background.*

Among the Classic period Maya centers, Copán was the first one selected for intensive excavations and sculpture recording by Harvard's Peabody Museum, just as it had been the first site that Maudslay excavated, the first that Stephens and Catherwood visited, and the first in which excavations were carried out and reported by Juan Galindo in 1834. It was also the first site to be exhaustively studied in the field by Morley. Not only did he document and analyze Copán's hieroglyphs, but he also studied the importance of other archaeological remains in the valley. The reason for all this interest is simple: Copán has more hieroglyphic inscriptions and other sculpted monuments than any other Maya ruin, or any other site in the New World, for that matter.

An examination of Catherwood's illustrations gives one a feeling for the ruins of Copán as well as an appreciation of the elaboration and intricacy of its sculpture. Indeed, the sculptors of Copán succeeded where most of their contemporaries failed, achieving such depth of relief that in many cases the human figures are almost in the round. It was an art style that appealed to Western aesthetics, with its appreciation of naturalism and movement. Given the preponderance of datable inscriptions, the clearly delineated and chronologically diagnostic styles, and the sheer abundance of sculptures at Copán – including thousands of surface fragments which originally adorned mosaic sculpture façades on the Acropolis temples and other important

II *View over the Ballcourt, with the Hieroglyphic Stairway visible on the right of the picture.*

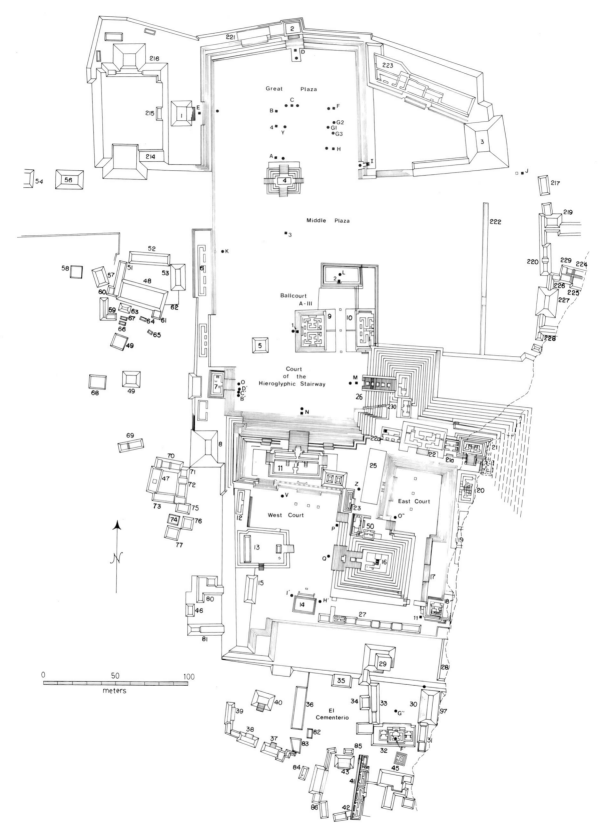

8 The Principal Group of ruins, showing the areas referred to in the text.

9 *The Great Plaza, looking south–southeast, with Ballcourt A-III and the Hieroglyphic Stairway in the background. Structure 10L-4, which defines the southern limit of the Great Plaza, has four stairways, in keeping with rituals related to the four cardinal directions.*

buildings – it is small wonder that Copán's stature and importance in the field grew as time passed.

The 'Principal Group' of ruins, or 'site core' in contemporary technical terminology, consists of a series of large buildings constructed around open courtyards (plazas), which frequently contain stelae and altars. Covering an area of 12 ha, the Principal Group consists of two basic parts: to the north, the open expanses of low-lying plazas; to the south, the enclosed and upraised courtyards and constituent structures built upon the area known since the turn of the century as the 'Acropolis' (a misnomer, since the mass upon which the final phase of building rests is not a natural hill but rather the build up of centuries of sequential construction – each king literally built upon the works of his predecessors).

Within these two areas, there are internal divisions. The low-lying north section comprised the Great Plaza with its magnificent stelae, the Middle Plaza where people entered the Principal Group along paved roads from east and west, and the Hieroglyphic Stairway Plaza on the south from which visitors could watch the activities taking place at the Ballcourt, at the Hieroglyphic

Stairway (of Structure 10L-26), and at the massive 'Temple of the Inscriptions' (Structure 10L-11). The Acropolis represents the superimposed constructions of over 400 years of Copán history and corporate labor projects. In the final phase, the structures presently visible were laid out around two large courtyards, labeled the East and West Courts. To the south of these are a series of elaborate élite residential structures, given the misleading name 'The Cemetery' by the modern villagers of Copán, after investigations by the Carnegie Institution yielded numerous burials of the people who had resided in this sector.

The Great Plaza is a large open area enclosed by steps (on the north, east and west) and by Structure 10L-4 (on the south), a building with a large stairway on each of its four sides. Within its confines are some of the finest examples of sculpture ever carved in the New World. The steps were not designed merely for access to the structures on the raised north, east, and west perimeters of the Great Plaza, but rather as seating areas – bleachers – for the spectators who came to watch the important public events of their day.

The stelae within the Great Plaza are among the most elaborate and high-relief examples of their kind ever produced by the Classic Maya. These stelae and their associated altars were all carved during the reign of the distinguished and long-lived 13th ruler of Copán – whose hieroglyphic name reads '18 Rabbit' – though stelae in honor of two of his ancestors were left in place on the east and west sides of the steps. In turn, his successors in office left intact 18 Rabbit's monuments in the coliseum-like Great Plaza, adding only three relatively inconspicuous altars (G1, G2, and G3) in the large space left between the two stelae on the east side of the original composition.

The Middle Plaza comprises a vast open space connected at its eastern and western extremities to the two roadways providing the principal means of access to the Principal Group during the Classic period. Indeed, the modern visitor walks along the western artery, much as workers, dignitaries, and pilgrims did in ancient times. The Middle Plaza has but a single monolith, a grandiose if badly-weathered example of a two-figured stela, this one carved on the most famous day in the life of the longest-lived and perhaps single most accomplished Copán dynast, the 12th ruler known as 'Smoke Imix God K' or 'Smoke Jaguar'. There was access from the Middle Plaza to the Great Plaza on its north, or to the Court of the Hieroglyphic Stairway, and thence to the Acropolis, on the south.

The Hieroglyphic Stairway Plaza is the smallest of the three north area plazas, but in many ways the most impressive, owing to the imposing nature of the architectural monuments which define its limits. To its north is the final version of Copán's main ballcourt (known as Ballcourt A-III), the largest of its kind from the southern lowlands, and one of the most elaborately embellished

10 (Opposite) The Hieroglyphic Stairway of Structure 10L-26, as restored by the Carnegie Institution. In this 1987 photo, Barbara Fash is visible two-thirds of the way up the stairway, in the process of drawing the inscription. At the foot of the stairway stands Stela M, bearing the likeness of the stairway's patron, the 15th ruler, Smoke Shell.

11 *Altar Q, west side. The left-central figure represents the revered founder of the Copán dynasty (Yax K'uk Mo'), passing a scepter of office to the right-central figure (Yax Pac), the 16th (and last) ruler in that dynasty. Yax K'uk Mo's name appears in his headdress, while all the other figures are identified by the hieroglyphs they sit upon. (Yax K'uk Mo' sits upon the glyph for 'lord'.) The date of Yax Pac's accession to power (6 Caban 10 Mol or 2 July 763) is shown between the two central figures. On the far left sits the 2nd ruler; on the far right sits the 15th ruler, Smoke Shell.*

12 *Altar Q, south side. The figures are shown in reverse chronological order, from left to right: ruler 14 (Smoke Monkey); ruler 13 (18 Rabbit); ruler 12 (Smoke Imix God K, shown seated on the glyph '5 Katun', indicating that he lived into his eighties); and ruler 11 (Butz' Chan).*

13 *Altar Q, east side. From left to right: ruler 10 (Moon Jaguar); ruler 9; ruler 8; ruler 7 (Waterlily Jaguar). The 8th and 9th rulers reigned for a combined total of only nine years, whereas both Moon Jaguar and Waterlily Jaguar enjoyed lengthy reigns.*

Altar Q

14 *Altar Q, north side. From left to right: ruler 6; ruler 5; ruler 4 (Cu Ix); ruler 3 (Mat Head). The 3rd and 4th rulers are cited in inscriptions at Quiriguá, as well as Copán; little is known of the 5th and 6th rulers.*

anywhere in Mesoamerica. Comprising two parallel buildings with a central playing alley between them, the main ballcourt served as the setting for the most public – and risk-laden – rubber ballgames played in ancient Copán.

On its east side (the most sacred direction in ancient Maya cosmography) is the Hieroglyphic Stairway and temple of Structure 10L-26, containing the official dynastic history and portraits of the Copán kings, dedicated by the 15th ruler, 'Smoke Shell', whose own portrait appears on the face of Stela M, placed at the bottom of the stairway.

On the south side of the plaza is the massive Structure 10L-11, the final version of which was crowned by a huge, two-storied temple boasting the greatest number of façade sculptures and inscribed hieroglyphic panels (eight in total) in Copán, thus its name – Temple of the Inscriptions. Built by the 16th ruler of Copán, known as 'Yax Pac' (First Dawn), Structure 10L-11's temple carries the largest single version of the Maya cosmogram known, on the north façade of the building, looking down on the aforementioned three plazas. To people coming into the Principal Group from the countryside, the visual impact of this structure must have been compelling indeed.

The steps up both Structure 10L-11 and Structure 10L-26 both give access to the raised portion of the Principal Group known since the turn of the century as the Acropolis. The north side of Structure 10L-11 itself faced the West Court of the Acropolis, with the lower portion actually touching the court known as the 'Reviewing Stand', containing another inscription dating to the reign of Yax Pac. On the east side of the West Court is the large pyramid-temple known as Structure 10L-16, with its temple doorway and frontal stairway both facing the West Court. At its foot was placed the famous Altar Q. Originally thought to represent an astronomer conference, Altar Q is now known to be a king list for the main ruling house of Copán. Commemorated by the 16th in the line of succession, the sides of the altar contain portraits and glyphic names of all the rulers of the dynasty traced to the early 5th-century ruler K'inich Yax K'uk Mo' (First – or Blue-green – Quetzal Macaw).[3]

The East Court of the Acropolis, like the Great Plaza, has a series of bleacher-like steps defining its east and north sides, but unlike the latter also has a sculpture-embellished 'reviewing stand' like that of the north side of Structure 10L-11. The East Court Reviewing Stand is found on the west side of the courtyard, and is embellished with snarling jaguars and the Jaguar Sun God of the Underworld. The steps on the north and east sides served as seating space and also provided access to a number of structures: 10L-17, 10L-18, 10L-19, 10L–20, 10L-21, 10L-21A, 10L-22, and 10L-22A. The elaborate and distinctive sculpture adornments on these structures indicate that they all had discrete meanings, and possibly different uses, in ancient times. The best-preserved and most often-remarked of these is Structure 10L-22 or 'Temple 22', containing in its inner chamber one of the finest examples of high-relief Maya sculpture ever produced. This, like the stelae of the Great Plaza, was also carved during the reign of the 13th ruler, 18 Rabbit.

The Copán Valley

Sylvanus Morley was the first to study Copán in a wider context, pointing out the importance of the other archaeological remains in the valley. He noted that the Principal Group in the center of the valley did not exist in isolation. There were thousands of other archaeological remains scattered throughout its 13-km length. He also noted that important temple complexes were found at several other sites, some of them including structures once adorned with beautiful sculptural mosaics. Morley even went so far as to predict that future research would demonstrate that almost the entire valley 'was one continuous settlement, one city'.[4]

In the modern epoch of Maya studies, largely owing to the example of Gordon Willey of Harvard University, archaeologists have shifted their research focus to the population that supported the rulers and their court, and the environmental backdrop that enabled that population to grow. Willey was the pioneer of the archaeological study of human settlement patterns. By studying the way a human population distributes itself and its resources on the landscape, one may come to know its size, level of organization, economic pursuits, defensive measures against its neighbors, and other social, economic, and political data. Rather than considering only the pyramids, temples, and palaces at the centers of Classic Maya settlements, archaeologists now attempt to map and, where possible, excavate the more humble remains of the supporting population.

In 1974 Willey was invited by the Honduran government to conduct an intensive study of Copán and its surrounding region. His primary goal was to produce an accurate and detailed map of the settlements, agricultural features (terraces, dams, etc.) and other evidence of human use of the landscape. The results of Willey's project, together with more recent research carried out at the site core and its sustaining area by a host of scholars in the Proyecto Arqueologico Copán (PAC), makes Copán the most thoroughly investigated of all the Classic Maya sites. Modern archaeology, with its emphasis on tightly-focused research problems, is well served by a site which has been investigated by distinguished specialists in virtually every aspect: hieroglyphic decipherment; art; architecture; ceramics; stone tools; environmental studies; settlement and land-use patterns; and population history, demography and disease (interpreted from human skeletal remains). With each passing year the problems that are addressed reach a level of sophistication that few would have predicted even ten short years ago.

The Copán Valley contains a wide variety of different environmental zones, ranging from steep hills and mountains up to 800 m, through gently rolling foothills and ancient high river terraces to the fertile low river terrace and floodplain at 600 m. The valley is clearly defined by the crests of its surrounding hills and mountains, and one would be remiss not to emphasize its sheer natural beauty. The hills and mountains make for a magnificent natural setting, a fact surely appreciated by its ancient inhabitants. Within its approximately 24 square kilometers grew the city of Copán.

For the Maya, the sacred importance of the hills and mountains lay in the fact that there were numerous caves hidden in their recesses. Since the most ancient times, caves were considered by all the peoples of Mesoamerica as a passage to the Underworld, the domain of the ancestral spirits and supernatural forces that determined the course of events on the surface world.

15 The Copán emblem-glyph. The beads on the left represent blood, and the two signs on the top read ah-po or ahau; together they signify that the person who carried the title was the 'blood lord' of that kingdom. In this case, the kingdom is named by a leaf-nosed bat, shown in profile.

Perhaps for this reason, the main element of the hieroglyph which names the ancient kingdom of Copán is the leaf-nosed bat, denizen of the sacred caves and of the Underworld.[5] Today the Copán Valley has an idyllic quality, but we must remember that the valley bottomlands were once lush and tropical, fraught with all the risks and dangers of those richly variegated environments. For the modern visitor, however, the remnants of forest, the caves, and the bats are but one aspect of an enchanting and picturesque environment. It is an admirable backdrop within which to attempt to put back the pieces of the archaeological puzzle that is ancient Copán.

Piecing together history

The puzzle metaphor was first used to describe Copán by Tatiana Proskouriakoff, the brilliant architect, artist, and epigrapher who was to forever change the field of Maya studies. Writing shortly after her first visit to Copán, Proskouriakoff bemoaned the fact that 'the beautifully carved fragments of its buildings lie scattered on the slopes of its pyramids like the pieces of a gigantic jigsaw puzzle in stone.'[6] This is the result of one clear disadvantage that the occupants of the Copán Valley faced: the relative paucity of limestone from which to make good-quality lime mortar for their constructions. Whereas the geological shelf of the Yucatán Peninsula provided limestone without limit for the occupants of most of the other Classic Maya sites, the Copán Valley and a few other places did not have this advantage. Thus, although lime was used for

16 Reconstruction painting by Tatiana Proskouriakoff of the Principal Group, much as it appeared at the time of Copán's apogee in the late 8th century AD. The Great Plaza is on the left, Ballcourt A-III and the Hieroglyphic Stairway of Structure 10L-26 in the center, and the Acropolis on the right. To the far right, the buildings of the 'Cemetery' residential area are visible.

plastering floors and exterior surfaces of masonry buildings at Copán, its relative scarcity promoted the use of mud mortar to hold together the buildings' rubble fills. Once the buildings were abandoned, the plaster cap on top of the structures cracked, enabling water and trees to penetrate the fill, eventually resulting in the collapse of at least the upper half of all the ruined buildings there. In addition, the devastating effects of periodic earthquakes have further reduced the once regal temples and palaces to rubble.

The collapse of the sculpture-embellished Copán building façades, then, poses a formidable challenge. Worse yet, for this particular puzzle there is no key from which one can base the reconstruction of elaborate structures which in three known instances originally boasted over 5000 fragments of mosaic façade sculpture. Compounding the problem is the fact that many sculptures have been moved from their original positions, both in ancient and modern times. Maudslay, in 1885, complained bitterly about the degree to which the

Introductory glyph ('In the count of days')	Tzapah ('was erected')
9 Baktuns (9 periods of 144,000 days)	Lin Chanil (proper name of Stela B)
15 Katuns (15 periods of 7200 days)	U bah mo' witz' ('he did it, macaw mountain')
0 Tuns (0 'years' of 360 days)	Ahau ('Lord')
0 Uinals (0 months of 20 days)	Completion
0 Kins (0 days)	15 Katuns
4 Ahau (260-day calendar date)	'He scattered drops' (bloodletting rite)
13 Yax (365-day calendar date)	U bah ('he did it')
Mitzil ('Invoked' or 'appeared')	Name of god he personifies
Chanal ch'u ('Heavenly god')	God K and other royal titles
Mitzil ('Invoked' or 'appeared')	13 hel, 'founder' (13th in the succession from the founder)
Kabal ch'u ('Earthly god')	18 'his smoke rodent' (XVIII Jog or 18 Rabbit)
Mitzil Venus god ('Invoked' Venus god)	Holy lord of Copán (the 'emblem-glyph')
Unknown	

The Maya system of time-reckoning

The Long Count represents a linear system of time-reckoning used in much of Mesoamerica from at least as early as the Late Preclassic period until the end of the 9th century AD, its fall from use marking the end of the Classic period in Maya history. The system records the time passed since a starting or 'zero' date, which modern scholars believe to have fallen on 13 August 3114 BC. Dates are given using progressively higher orders of days, beginning with a *kin* (one day) and progressing to a *baktun* (144,000 days) as follows:

20 *kins*   = 1 *uinal* (20 days)
18 *uinals* = 1 *tun* (360 days)
20 *tuns*   = 1 *katun* (7,200 days)
20 *katuns* = 1 *baktun* (144,000 days)

Each date is recorded in the form of five numbers (e.g. 8.7.3.17.3 or 8 *baktuns*, 7 *katuns*, 3 *tuns*, 17 *uinals*, and 3 *kins*), the total being the number of days elapsed since the zero date in 3114 BC.

In Classic Maya inscriptions, complete Long Count dates are preceded by an introductory glyph, and often followed by the position of that date in the other time counts they used: the 260-day ritual calendar or *Tzolkin* (combining 13 numbers and 20 named days, with the same number and day – e.g. '4 Ahau' – repeating once every 260 days); the 365-day solar or 'vague year' calendar or *Haab* (comprising 18 months of 20 days, plus an unlucky month of 5 days at the end); a sequential count of the 9 'Lords of the Night', following each other sequentially in endless succession; a lunar count (giving the lunar month, day in the lunation, and length of lunation); and occasionally another ritual calendar of 819 days. The sum total of all these time counts in Classic Maya inscriptions is known as the 'Initial Series', based on their position at the beginning of any inscription they appear in.

Most Initial Series texts refer to dates of historical importance falling in the lifetimes of the Classic Maya rulers (see Stela B, Copán, presented here). But some Long Count dates (which Floyd Lounsbury has called 'manipulated dates') refer to supernatural events, in the past and the future, and are supposed to justify the acts of Maya rulers that fell on days normally considered inappropriate for such purposes, or that broke with traditional behavior. In the case illustrated here, the Long Count date (transcribed as 9.15.0.0.0 and corresponding to 8 August AD 731) is followed by a passage describing the commemoration of this named monument. The ceremony celebrated the passage of a major 'Period Ending' (the completion of 15 *katuns* during the 9th *baktun*, some 1,404,000 days since the beginning of the Long Count), with the ritual 'scattering' (probably of the ruler's own blood), that often accompanied such important calendric anniversaries. Such Period Endings occurred every 5 *tuns* in the Long Count, and were one of the most common times for the commemoration of hieratic art and inscriptions. Sometimes other ceremonies besides 'scattering' were performed on these anniversaries, but the letting of the ruler's own blood seems to have been the most precious offering he could provide to his gods and his ancestors on these momentous occasions.

17 (Opposite) *The Initial Series of Stela B, with the Long Count date 9.15.0.0.0 (AD 731).*

sculptures had been moved about the site. What he did not know was that nearly 100 years later archaeologists would prove that this practice was an ancient one, having been practiced even before the end of the Classic period!

Fortunately, the prospects for puzzling out the temples are not wholly discouraging. First, it seems that each Copán structure was designed and decorated to distinguish it from all others at the site: thus, motifs are specific to each building. Second, in Copán the sculptures were in most cases carved *after* the stone blocks had been set into the façade of the structure, making it possible to line up adjacent pieces of the same motif complex on the basis of shared lines and depth of relief. Third, the techniques of modern archaeology, when rigorously applied to the excavation of sculpture-adorned structures, yield crucial contextual and structural evidence. Last, but certainly not least, the combined insights of epigraphers, artists, archaeologists, architects, and art historians are crucial for putting the Copán monuments back together again. Reconstructing the form, decoration, and stratigraphic associations of Copán architecture allows one in many cases to date the buildings within the newly reconstructed dynastic history of the site, and to gain a greater appreciation of their meaning to the ancient Maya.

The Copán Mosaics Project, under the author's direction, has been dedicated to precisely this process, the present book being among the first vehicles for publishing the results.

Perhaps the single most fascinating puzzle being pieced back together is that of the written history of Copán, as reconstructed by the arduous and creative work of the project epigraphers. Besides deciphering the elegant Long Count dates and the abbreviated 'Calendar Round' dates that have been the focus of Maya hieroglyphic studies since the 19th century, modern scholars have followed two new paths of decipherment. The 'historical approach', spawned by the works of Tatiana Proskouriakoff and Heinrich Berlin, analyzes Classic Maya inscriptions to establish the names and genealogy of the individuals cited, their relations with other kingdoms, and the important historical events depicted in the texts. The 'phonetic approach', first championed by the early 19th-century scholar Cyrus Thomas, was revived in the 1950s by the Russian scholar Yurii Knorosov at about the same time that Proskouriakoff and Berlin were making their breakthroughs in interpreting the historical code. This approach focuses on the actual decipherment of the phonetic value of specific signs, and is based on: an 'alphabet' of the sounds of the Spanish language recorded in Maya script by a 16th-century Maya scribe; the substitution of signs in different versions of a glyph with known meaning; and the comparison of modern and ancient Mayan languages.

All scholars now agree that besides recording dates in the Long Count, the solar and lunar calendars, and the various ritual and planetary calendars, the Classic Maya stone inscriptions record actual historical events. These events are identified by specialized hieroglyphs recording verbs (originally called 'event glyphs' by Proskouriakoff) which follow directly after the dates on the

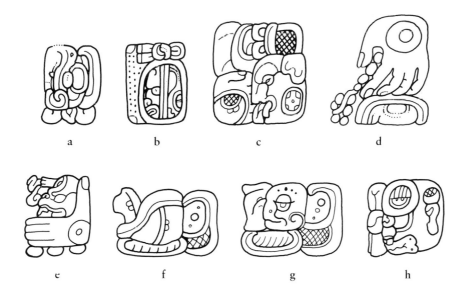

18 Often-cited verbs in Classic Maya inscriptions: *a* birth; *b* and *c* accession to power; *d* 'scattering' rite performed on Period Ending dates; *e* 'manikin scepter in hand' ceremony, performed on accessions and Period Endings; *f* capture; *g* burial; *h* death.

texts. Careful documentation, contextual analysis, and comparative study indicate that the verbs include those for birth, accession to power, genealogy, royal visits, marriage, war and the capture of rivals, death, and burial. A particularly frequent verb is the sign for 'scattering', a ritual performed by the ruler on the important 'Period Endings', occurring every five years.

Following the verbs in the inscriptions are the names of the protagonists of those actions, the actors on the stage of Classic Maya history. The proper name of these individuals usually takes up one or two glyph blocks, and is often followed by a series of other name glyphs referred to variously as 'titles' or 'attributes'. The final such title in the often lengthy name clauses is a specialized sign first recognized by Berlin. This glyph has certain core elements found at all sites, but the main sign was distinctive, and diagnostic, for each Maya site. Berlin concluded that each site or kingdom (or possibly its ruling lineage) had its own distinctive hieroglyph, which he called the 'emblem-glyph'. Thus, even if the protagonist's name is eroded on a Classic Maya inscription, so long as the emblem-glyph survives one knows where the individual harks from.

The amount of erosion and purposeful destruction of the Classic period monuments means that the need for such detective work is commonplace. Epigraphers can reconstruct the complete date of a monument, or the name of the ruler, or the event cited in the text, on the basis of the well-preserved clues from the inscription under study, as well as from the study of other texts which carry the same references. Once a ruler's inaugural (or 'accession') and death dates are known, monuments within his domain can be attributed to his reign based on their date, or citation of that dynast as the protagonist of the event commemorated by the text. The cumulative nature of hieroglyphic decipherment often enables epigraphers to fill out a dynastic sequence from a given site on the basis of partial or badly eroded hieroglyphic inscriptions.

Despite strong resistance during the first half of this century, there is now a consensus that the Maya writing system was a mixed script that combined pictographic and phonetic elements. Some disagreement continues on the amount and degree of phoneticism in the script, but most scholars agree that the decipherment of the phonetic elements holds the future for the actual reading of the script in the spoken words of the ancient Maya. The phonetic approach has allowed for the reading of the names of the makers of Classic Maya history, and for such previously unknown subjects as place-names and monument names. Work on decipherment continues at such a blistering pace that the published word cannot hope to keep up with it. Important new decipherments will continue to be made at Copán and elsewhere in the years ahead.

In the meantime, productive research on the valley settlements continues to be carried out by David Webster and William Sanders and their students, and by Wendy Ashmore of Rutgers University and her students. These investigations tell us more about the people who made up the social fabric of ancient Copán, and help us to understand the context within which the rulers acted. These data are of critical importance in understanding the direction of change in the public monuments of the Principal Group of ruins. If we know under what conditions the rulers were operating, we may be able to deduce why they produced the monuments they did. We must not forget that the larger, more public buildings and statuary that the Classic Maya produced were essentially politico-religious advertisements, designed to communicate information to the masses in the service of political ends. On the one hand, we seek to understand why people nucleated and evolved a non-egalitarian society by studying the ideological and political forces which generated or justified those changes. On the other, we aspire to comprehend the nature of the political and religious symbols developed and used by the élites of Maya society by thoroughly scrutinizing the material remains of the population called upon to produce those symbols on a grand scale.

So much has been written about Copán, and the story is so complex, that I can only hope to touch upon some of the high points in the pages that follow. But I also hope to be able to impart some of the sense of excitement and discovery felt by the numerous scholars who have labored and triumphed in pursuit of the past in these magnificent ruins for some 150 years.

III *The scarlet macaw on Structure 10L-10 of Ballcourt A-III, as restored in 1988 by the Copán Mosaics Project.*

IV *The Great Plaza, with the stela of the ruler 18 Rabbit in the foreground.*

CHAPTER TWO

THE COPÁN VALLEY AND ITS ENVIRONMENT

Incentives for settlement

Nestled between volcanic cliffs and sedimentary hills in western Honduras, the Copán River has carved out a series of small valleys or 'pockets' containing some of the richest soils in Central America. Even today, Copán is famous for the quality of its tobacco, which is one of the most nitrogen-demanding of all crops. Studies of ancient river geomorphology show that until about the 8th century A D, annual flooding of the valley bottomlands made for the renewal of already fertile and mostly well-drained soils: the perfect situation for a population which practiced agriculture as its main form of subsistence. In the 1860s this very fertility attracted numerous settlers into the Copán Valley from adjacent parts of Guatemala, who set about clearing the forest in order to farm the land. As a result, the Copán region has been cleared of the tropical forest cover prevalent in Stephens' day, making it considerably easier than in most of the rest of the Maya lowlands to find, map, and excavate the remains of the ancient buildings and other cultural features.

Another environmental advantage which the Copán Valley inhabitants had was access to various abundant raw materials. The green volcanic tuff used for dressed stone in buildings and for sculptures, outcrops throughout the valley, including one very large vein found 0.5 km north of the Principal Group. This stone is geologically stable in the region, and thus the sculptures of Copán, when not battered by falling from their original positions, are generally found in a remarkably good state of preservation, including details critical for studying them in depth. The largest known source of jade in Mesoamerica is within three days' walk of Copán in the Middle Motagua Valley, in what is now eastern Guatemala. And at a distance of 80 km was a source of obsidian – the nearly transparent volcanic glass used by the Maya and many other ancient peoples for making stone tools – at the outcrop of Ixtepeque. (Obsidian tools have been found in virtually all ancient households in the valley. This is a great boon to the modern archaeologist, for the hydration layer on the edge of a tool can be used for dating it. The longer the obsidian artifact is buried, the more water it absorbs and the thicker the 'hydration layer' that forms on the tool's edges. The rate of this hydration process is calculated by measuring with polarized light the thickness of the layer found on obsidian tools from dated contexts. Having established the hydration rate, one can then calculate a date

V *Stela H, the best preserved and most beautiful stela at Copán. Formerly believed to portray a woman, it is now thought to be a portrait of 18 Rabbit, in a skirt.*

for virtually any piece of obsidian found in an excavation, based on the thickness of its hydration layer. This in turn allows one to date the use of the buildings and other features with which the stone tools are associated, helping to elucidate the history of the settlement and land-use in the valley.)

A granite outcrop in the eastern end of the valley was exploited to make the grinding stones necessary for processing maize kernels into flour for making tortillas and other foods. A kaolin source north of the valley was used for manufacturing and decorating pottery. There were several small limestone outcrops from which lime could be produced, and the river brought other useful kinds of stones (including flint for producing chipped stone tools) from outcrops in the mountains higher upstream.

In sharp contrast to the flat, limestone shelf that forms the physical setting for the vast majority of the Classic Maya centers, the region in which the ruins of Copán are located constitutes a highly varied landmass. In fact, geographically (and to a certain extent culturally), Copán is more highland than lowland.[1] In large part due to its elevation of approximately 600 m, the mean annual temperature of the Copán Valley is 78°F, considerably milder than most of the rest of the Maya lowlands. Also unlike the other lowland areas, the Copán region is characterized by a marked change in seasons, with a dry season running from January to the end of May, and a rainy season extending from June to the end of December. This is unlike the tropical forest of the southern lowlands, said by many to have only a 'wet' season, and a 'wetter' season, and also unlike the Peninsula of Yucatán, where rain is scarce even in the wet season. The Copán River provides ample water all year, whereas surface water is relatively scarce in Yucatán and parts of the Petén (south of Yucatán). The Copán River was responsible for carving out areas of fertile, level land that were the initial impetus for the settling of this region by incipient agriculturalists in the latter half of the first millennium BC.

The Copán River and its works

The Copán River cuts westward through the mountainous regions of far western Honduras and adjacent eastern Guatemala, before debouching into the Motagua River north of the modern Guatemalan city of Zacapa. The river is variously called the Río Amarillo, the Río Copán, or the Río Camotán in its upper, middle, and lower courses. It originates in the Sierra Gallinero, which separates the Copán drainage system from that of the Chamelecón River drainage, the latter flowing north and east to the vast Sula Plain and the north coast of Honduras. The Copán River flows in a sinewy fashion, running some 38 km (27 km in straight-line distance) before entering Guatemala. Along the way it acquires the flow of other rivers and streams, some permanent, others intermittent, such as the Río Blanco, the Río Mirasol, the Río Gila, and the *quebradas* (ravines) of Otuta, Quebradona, Seca, and Sesesmil. Many of these tributaries have their sources in mountain springs.

19 Map of western Honduras and the adjacent part of southeastern Guatemala, showing the principal pockets of the Copán River system and the location of Quiriguá, Río Amarillo, El Paraiso, Los Higos, and the obsidian source, Ixtepeque.

The topography of the Copán drainage system is in general quite rugged, with most of the tributaries cutting through sharp escarpments before reaching the more level bed of the Río Copán itself. In the 22 km from its source, at an elevation of 1100 m, to the Principal Group of ruins, the river descends some 500 m. There are a number of rapids along its course, which would have made canoe travel difficult. In the Honduras portion of its length it has gouged out a series of small areas of open, level lands. The term 'pocket' has been used to refer to the sections of alluvial plains which have been formed by the river in this way.[2] Out of respect for traditional usage, most students have maintained the use of the term 'Copán Valley' (which should not be confused with the Copán basin or drainage system) to refer to the Copán *pocket* of the Copán

Valley *system*. The Copán pocket contains the Principal Group of ruins and its immediately adjacent settlements, which are much greater in size and number than those found in the other pockets. From east to west, the pockets on the Honduran side of the system are named Upper (or east) Río Amarillo, Lower (or west) Río Amarillo, El Jaral, Santa Rita, and Copán.

Of these small valleys or pockets, the Copán pocket is the largest and most open, measuring nearly 6 km at its widest point (from ridge to ridge), and about 12.5 km in length, following the river. Its alluvial bottomlands cover an area of 10.3 sq. km. The three pockets immediately east of the Copán pocket are much smaller, with only 6 sq. km of alluvial bottomlands. The eastern-most pocket, Upper Río Amarillo, is nearly the size of the Copán pocket, with 8.8 sq. km of level alluvial lands, formed by the Río Blanco and the upper-most course of the Copán River (here called the Río Amarillo). Besides the major pockets of bottomlands carved out by the Copán River, there are also smaller patches of level lands along some of the tributary drainages. These are referred to as 'intermontaine pockets', and evidence of ancient settlements has been found in each of them. None approach the size or density of occupation found in the settlements of the pockets of the Copán River itself.

These five small areas are each characterized by four types of landforms, all of which are very well represented in the Copán pocket. These consist of floodplains, alluvial terraces, foothills, and steeply-sloping hills and mountains. The floodplains are generally rather restricted in size, with most of the bottomlands comprising alluvial terraces. An exception is Upper Río Amarillo, where there is a rather large floodplain. Unfortunately this large expanse of floodplain has exceptionally poor drainage, making for permanently waterlogged soils.

Of the five pockets, the Copán pocket is distinguished not only by its extensive bottomlands, but also by its relatively large expanses of foothills zones. The foothills grade into the steeper slopes higher up, with the gradation being particularly smooth in the eastern sector of the valley. Copán pocket foothills contain a series of ancient alluvial terraces, referred to as 'high river terraces', as opposed to the 'low river terraces' which make up the majority of the valley bottomlands. Besides the high river terraces formed by the ancient Copán River, there is also a series of alluvial fans, formed over hundreds of thousands of years by the tributary streams, which flow into the river in the Copán pocket. The modern town of Copán rests atop one such alluvial fan, formed long ago by the Quebrada Sesesmil. These larger expanses of gently rolling terrain, in tandem with a larger, better-drained section of alluvial bottomlands, made the Copán pocket a considerably more attractive place for settlement by an agricultural population than any of the adjacent pockets.

In addition to physiographic variation between the five pockets, there is considerable variation in climate. The three eastern pockets are higher up and closer to the source of most of the rainfall for this region (the Sierra Gallinero), and have a cooler climate and higher mean annual precipitation, than do the

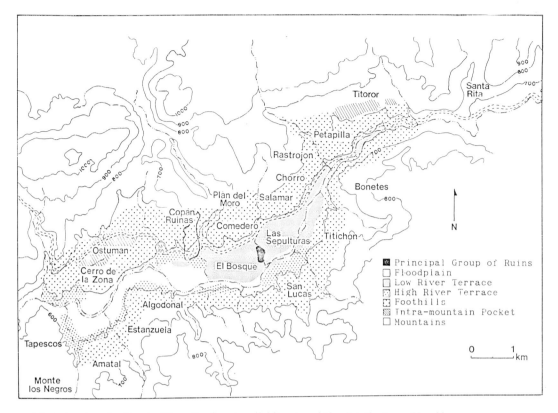

20 Map showing the Copán River (broken parallel lines) and the distribution of landforms and modern place-names in the Copán pocket.

two western pockets. Indeed, as one proceeds downward and westward into Guatemala from the Copán pocket, the temperature, precipitation, and vegetation regimes alter dramatically, leading into the drier, more desert-like zone of the Middle Motagua River basin. The El Jaral pocket, for example, has a mean annual precipitation of 1700 mm, whereas the figures available for the Copán pocket record a mean of only 1439 mm. Further west, not only does the amount of precipitation decrease, but the year-to-year fluctuations in precipitation dramatically increase. This means that for the area west of the Copán pocket, there was (and still is) a greater degree of risk that any given year will bring more, or less, rainfall than required for agriculture.

The Copán pocket thus has tremendous natural advantages over its neighbors in terms of size, amount of well-drained bottomland soils, extent and fertility of its foothills zones, and amount and regularity of rainfall. The cultural geographer B.L. Turner II and his associates noted that it was in fact on an 'ecotone', that is, a zone of relatively rapid transition in vegetation. To the west extend the dry regions of eastern Guatemala, and to the east is the more tropical vegetation of Río Amarillo and its environs.

Geological history and distribution of arable land

The geological history of the valley, worked out by Gail Mahood of Stanford University, begins in the Cretaceous period (136–64 million years ago), with the deposit of blue-grey limestones and fine-grained maroon-red siltstones.[3] The whole area was then subjected to uplift, raising many of the originally horizontal beds to vertical positions. Further sedimentation later occurred during the Early Tertiary period (from 64 million years ago).

Much later, cycles of intense volcanic activity (resulting in the deposition of tuffs from burning clouds of ash and pumice), and the action of the river which subsequently cut through this tuff, produced layers of tuff and sediment that almost completely filled the valley. A final eruption about 10 million years ago was followed by a quieter geological phase, during which the river carved out the Tertiary fill, leaving only a few scattered crests of these ancient rocks. The river was then at a higher elevation than at present, and it built up at least two terraces, while the waters of the Quebrada Sesesmil were forming the large alluvial fan still seen today.

The result of these geological events and processes is the landscape we see today, and which the Maya occupied a geological instant ago. Outcrops of some of these stones were intensely utilized by the ancient Maya, particularly the finer and purer beds of limestone (to produce lime-plaster for construction and floors), the outcrops of tuff (for masonry buildings, stelae, altars, and architectural sculptures), and in all likelihood the chert outcrops interbedded with the limestone in Petapilla.

But the geological history also had other important effects on the use of the terrain, particularly with regard to soil formation. The soils deriving from the siltstones were (and are) very shallow and low in nutrients, whereas those deriving from the tuff deposits were slightly better for agriculture, and those forming on the surface of the limestone beds were better still. The very best soils, however, were those built up in alluvial terraces by the Copán River itself, as it carved out the pockets of the Copán basin.

The areas used for intensive agriculture in the Copán Valley today are in all likelihood the same as those exploited in ancient times. It is highly unlikely that the upper slopes now covered with pine forests were ever used for agricultural purposes because of the low fertility and acidic nature of their soils. This idea seems to be borne out by the settlement data, since very few mounds or other relics of ancient activity or occupation have been found in these areas. Of the different kinds of soils found in the foothills and adjacent slopes, those which derive from limestone substrates, or those which constituted high alluvial terraces formed by the river were undoubtedly the most fertile and probably the ones most intensively cultivated. The alluvial soils on the low river terrace and in the floodplain were the most fertile of the region, comprising silts and clays laced with nutrients deposited during river floods. Today the Copán Valley bottomlands constitute some of the richest soils in Central America.

History of land-use in the valley

The river geomorphology and alluvial history of the Copán pocket was worked out by William Johnson of the University of Kansas by examining the escarpments of the river terraces and streams, and by detailed analysis of samples from test-pits excavated by the archaeologists of the PAC I.[4] Johnson was able to demonstrate that the surface and the escarpments of the high river terrace are pre-Maya, dating to the Late Pleistocene, *c.* 10,000 years ago. The entrenching of the river in the valley bottomlands apparently reached bedrock, and evidence of sedimentation of the valley bottom was found in pre-occupation levels in the deep test-pits dug on either side of the Principal Group, along the edges of the streams, and from auger samples of the soil. Sitting atop some of these buried alluvial soils are occupations dating to the Middle Preclassic, and in one case (at Group 9N-8, see Chapter Four) the last centuries of the Early Preclassic (*c.* 1300–1000 BC).

In Johnson's estimation, the bottomlands of the Copán River saw periodic aggradations as well as lateral movements of the river during the period from 1000 BC up to the beginning of the Middle Classic. It is difficult to evaluate the duration and the intensity of the aggradations, but it appears that although frequent they were not of great magnitude, and apparently did not produce significant cultural disturbances. The deep test-pits and other excavations conducted in the valley bottom generally show a sequence of fine sediments with cultural material and, occasionally, some cobble formations probably representing the fills of constructions. Distributed irregularly within these stratigraphic sequences one finds layers or lenses of sand, silt, or clay deposited by the river. The natural origin of these latter deposits was confirmed by composition analysis, but their limited horizontal extent and vertical depth indicates that they were not the result of catastrophic floods.

It appears that during the latter half of the Middle Classic, and certainly by AD 700, the Maya had diverted the Copán River in order to prevent further aggradation and lateral movement in the valley bottomlands. The manpower and technical expertise necessary to channel the river unquestionably existed by Middle Classic times, and the size of the population and its permanence in the valley bottom at that time would have made such a project highly desirable to all concerned (see Chapter Five). The area occupied by the Principal Group itself sits on an alluvial fan produced by the actions of the Quebrada Salamar and was apparently elevated and well protected enough to have been spared erosion, at least from the Middle Classic to the end of the Late Classic period.

Some time after the abandonment of the Principal Group, however, the man-made channel was wiped out by the river. Johnson estimates that some time between 1000 and 500 years ago, the river dug deeply into its own channel. In doing so it also gouged out the present floodplain, leaving the surface of the Classic period bottomlands high and dry: easily distinguishable from the floodplain and referred to by us as the low river terrace. This downtrenching of the Copán River was followed by a period of vertical stability, when the river stayed at the same elevation, but meandered, carving a wider floodplain. The result of this vertical stability was a most unfortunate one for the archaeologist, for the gouging out of the new floodplain resulted in the destruction of over 200 ha of the Classic-period landscape, including all the archaeological remains that had existed at those locations. The lateral cutting of the present floodplain destroyed a very large section of the terraces and structures on the east side of the Acropolis, producing the aptly named 'Archaeological Cut'. Indeed, despite numerous attempts to control the destructive force of the river at the end of the 19th century, in the first two decades of this century three buildings of the East Court of the Acropolis (Structures 10L-20, 10L-20A, and most of 10L-21) were completely carried away by the river.

But the Acropolis was only one of the features to be affected by the creation of the modern floodplain. Large sections of bottomlands which once supported densely-settled residential areas of the urban sector of Copán were also wiped out by the river. Particularly noteworthy and tragic losses occurred in the areas to the south of the extant remains of the Las Sepulturas and El Bosque wards of the city, where there must originally have been several hundred Late Classic structures, now completely washed away. It is likely that there were also many residential structures immediately south of the alluvial fan where the modern town sits, because we know that the top of the fan was densely settled in Late Classic times. Here too, the original Late Classic landscape was destroyed by the river. It seems ironic that the Copán River, the reason for settling this region in the first place, itself destroyed many of the settlements dating to the apogee of Classic Maya civilization in the Copán Valley. This fact must be taken into account when population figures are estimated for the valley (see Chapter Eight).

The diverse land-forms, different soil types, and distinct precipitation regimes of the Copán drainage basin doubtless made for a great deal of variation in the pre-Maya vegetation cover. However, owing to manipulation of the environment, both ancient and modern, there are at present only three basic types of forest cover: mixed seasonal deciduous forest (found in the valley bottomlands), high seasonal deciduous forest (found on the foothills), and pine–oak forest (on the upper slopes). When Galindo, and later Stephens and Catherwood, visited Copán in the first half of the 19th century, the bottomlands were covered in dense tropical forest, inhabited by monkeys and jaguars. This forest had grown in the area since the abandonment of ancient Copán, and included mahogany, chico zapote, ceiba, Spanish cedar, and large fig trees. In the 1860s immigrants from Guatemala, attracted by the fertility of the region, came into the Copán pocket and cut down the forest, leaving only a few giant ceibas and some large Spanish cedars in the area of the Acropolis. A delightful publication by Wilson Popenoe in 1919, entitled *The useful plants of Copán* lists all the plant species used by the early 20th-century occupants of the

21 View of the Copán Valley, with the Principal Group in the forested area in the foreground.

valley, including the staples of maize, beans, squash, and chile; fruits such as the avocado, cacao, zapote, jocote, pineapple, anona, guava, and papaya; non-edible species such as tobacco, and cotton; and a wealth of other, less well known plants.

Circumscription theory and agriculture

The clear delineation of the Copán Valley by hills and mountains makes this setting an ideal one for studies of ancient Maya culture change. The anthropologist Robert Carneiro has devised a theory for explaining the rise of complex culture and the 'state' level of socio-political integration, based on the principle of 'circumscription'.[5] According to Carneiro's theory, early states are most likely to develop in areas which are surrounded by geographical features impeding expansion of the population into previously unoccupied areas. Thus, for ancient Egypt, the Nile Valley was surrounded by desert and by the sea beyond the desert. The smaller the circumscribed area in which an agricultural society establishes itself, the sooner it is likely to develop social institutions that promote and protect a hierarchy of economic and political power. So, in the case of Copán the agricultural land concentrated in the alluvial bottomlands of the valley constituted the critical resource that would become the spark for increased competition and the generation of more complex social and political institutions. This geographic setting makes Copán one of the easiest Maya sites with which to test the circumscription theory, and other ecologically-based models for the explanation of culture change.

Studies of fossil pollen preserved in the Copán Valley were conducted by Frederick Wiseman in 1979, and by David Rue in 1985 and 1989. These studies show evidence for agricultural activity (especially maize cultivation) in the valley beginning *c.* 1000 BC, and continuing well beyond the end of the Classic period. It is believed that the basic type of agriculture practiced by the Classic Maya was the swidden or 'slash-and-burn' system still used in the Maya area today, where a patch of forest will be cleared and cultivated for two years or so, before the farmers move on to allow the soil to regenerate. The basic swidden system was improved upon in some areas of the Maya lowlands, particularly with the advent of raised fields and other methods of intensifying production, as early as the Late Preclassic period, in areas as far separated as Pulltrouser Swamp in Belize and the lowlands of Campeche around Edzná. In the Copán Valley, there is some evidence for the intensification of techniques in the form of dry stone terrace walls and water-control systems: diversion channels in the alluvial bottomlands were uncovered in excavation Operation IV/79; and a dam for water retention across a stream was found in Petapilla, but its antiquity is disputed. However, nothing has yet been found to match the labor intensity or the magnitude of production visible in true 'hydraulic societies', such as Teotihuacan and Tenochtitlan in Central Mexico. Instead, it appears that the Copán Maya were dependent upon basic rainfall agriculture, centered on the cultivation of maize, beans, and squash – the agricultural 'trinity' of ancient Mesoamerica – and supplemented by garden crops such as chile, tomatoes, and fruit trees. Today, double-cropping of maize and beans is possible in the wetter, upland reaches of the Copán drainage basin such as the Quebrada Sesesmil and Upper Río Amarillo pocket, and it is likely that it was practiced in ancient times, as well.

The question of the intensity and duration of agricultural practices in the Maya area has been a controversial one, and interpretation at Copán is no exception. Indeed, Rue's study of the fossil pollen helped alert archaeologists to the fact that the Copán Valley continued to be occupied and cultivated for at least three centuries after the political collapse of the centralized ruling order in the Principal Group of ruins.[6] Wiseman's study also indicated that the three basic forest types represented today, albeit in truncated form, were also present during the Classic period. There does not, therefore, appear to have been any significant difference between the present-day climate, and that of the Classic period. We will refer to the pollen studies again in our consideration of the collapse of the Copán city-state, but we will now turn to the way scholars have attempted over the years to answer this and other questions about Copán.

CHAPTER THREE

MAYA ARCHAEOLOGY COMES OF AGE

Soon after we had set to work [at Copán], war broke out between the Republics of Guatemala and Honduras on the one side and San Salvador and Nicaragua on the other. This war seriously interfered with my work . . . All the mules in the neighbourhood were taken up for war-transport, and there was much difficulty in getting up the relays of stores and material I needed from Yzabal. Nearly all my labourers were carried off to serve – very unwillingly – as soldiers, and my work had to be carried on with such men as had passed the military age, and a few waifs and strays who had managed to escape the vigilance of the government officers. Every now and then a report came that troops were marching towards the village, and my neighbours generally prepared to betake themselves to the bush with such few valuables as they possessed, and leave the village in charge of two or three cripples and some ancient ladies . . . My friends in the city of Guatemala wrote to me, most strongly urging me to beat a retreat to the coast, and added that it was quite impossible, in the dangerous state of the roads, to send me the silver I needed to continue paying my workmen. But I determined to hold on . . .[1]

Earliest archaeological adventures in Central America

Such was the situation in which the determined Englishman Alfred Percival Maudslay found himself in 1885, as he tried to carry out his investigations in the ruins and to make plaster casts of the Copán sculptures. It seems that not much had changed since the days of Stephens and Catherwood, who were arrested and thrown into jail by some undesirable characters on the road to Copán. Traveling in back-woods country in Central America in the 19th century, a time of great political upheaval in the wake of independence from Spain, was not to be taken lightly. The sheer grit and determination of such men as Maudslay, Galindo, Stephens and Catherwood, and the members of the Harvard University Peabody Museum Honduras Expedition, is nothing short of remarkable. Driven by curiosity and ambition, these individuals had to overcome any number of obstacles, from man and nature alike, to carry out their chosen mission. Truth to tell, however, many of their problems were of their own making. Stephens, for example, admitted that he knew virtually no Spanish, yet he undertook to untangle all the Byzantine politics of a region in political turmoil. Maudslay insisted on taking four tons of delicate plaster casts out of Copán on muleback at the height of later hostilities. Not to be outdone, the Peabody Museum made casts of each of the steps of the Hieroglyphic Stairway, also to be taken out on the ancient mountain trails ('never altered by the hands of man') via porter and muleback. It is perhaps because of the inhospitableness of the mountain trails, and the frontier nature of the Copán Valley in colonial New Spain geography, that such a wondrous ruin had been neglected for so long to begin with.

The first report on the archaeological site of Copán was written in 1576 by Diego García de Palacio, to Philip II, King of Spain. The details of the account given by García de Palacio leave no question but that he saw the ruins himself. Indeed, at the time of his visit six of the stelae of the Great Plaza were still standing, one more than the five still upright in Stephens' day. In 1576 there was a formal entrance to the city, 'and a great eagle in stone, having on its breast a tablet a yard square, and on it certain characters which are not understood'.[2] García de Palacio accurately described the Great Plaza, and several of the more important sculptures at the site, but was frustrated in his attempts to discern who, precisely, were the people responsible for this 'seat of great power and a great population, civilized and considerably advanced in the arts'.[3] The best he could discern from the natives (who, he makes a point of noting, did not have any books, though he himself had somehow managed to acquire one) was that 'They say that in ancient times there came from Yucatán a great lord who built these edifices, but that at the end of some years he returned to his native country, leaving them entirely deserted'.[4] García de Palacio reported that the name of the village or town where the ruins were located was Copán, and from that day forward the ruins have been known by that name. Unfortunately, Copán is unquestionably not the ancient name of the site. Other accounts of the ruins were written by Francisco Antonio Fuentes y Guzmán (in 1689) and by Domingo Juarros (in 1808), but these are so fanciful that most scholars doubt they actually visited the site themselves.

In April 1834 a Colonel Juan Galindo visited the ruins, acting under a commission from the government of Central America. Having already made explorations at the Maya ruins of Palenque and Utatlán, Galindo was uniquely qualified to make a study of the site of Copán. Although he spent several months at Copán writing notes and drawing plans, vistas, and renderings of the hieroglyphic texts, his report was never actually published until much later. But he did succeed in having several letters describing the ruins published in newspapers and literary journals of the day in London, Paris, and New York. He is also to be credited with effecting the first excavations at the site, conducted in the East Court of the Acropolis, where he found a tomb chamber containing a number of ceramic vessels filled with human bones.

Although brief and superficial, Galindo's descriptions caught the eye of John Lloyd Stephens, whose much more lengthy and well-illustrated account *Incidents of Travel in Central America, Chiapas, and Yucatán* (1841), became an instant bestseller, going through ten editions within three months of its original printing. Besides the spellbinding narrative, the book was blessed with superb illustrations by the English artist Frederick Catherwood. Catherwood's great talent was matched perhaps only by his tenacity: to read of the conditions in which he was obliged to produce his drawings makes one admire them all the more. Stephens alternates between moving passages of lament that nothing can be concluded about the makers or the meaning of the monuments on the one hand, and some very insightful observations and deductions on the other. Given his previous experience in documenting the ancient monuments of Egypt and the Near East, it was quite reasonable for Stephens to deduce the historical nature of the Classic Maya art and inscriptions. He also surmised that at least some of the altars placed in front of the stelae were used for sacrifice.

For sheer charm and high adventure, it is doubtful whether anything can match Stephens' narrative. Particularly incredible to us today is that he was able to secure the purchase of the ruins of Copán for a total of $50 US! 'There was never any difficulty about price. I offered that sum, for which Don José María thought me only a fool; if I had offered more, he would probably have considered me something worse.'[5]

Maudslay, the Peabody Museum, and the first scientific investigations

Although several individuals came to the ruins in the following decades, it was not until 1885 that another important chapter in the history of the exploration of Copán was opened. Alfred Percival Maudslay, after having previously made 'a journey of curiosity' to the Maya ruins, set about the business of making initial excavations, detailed plans, sections and maps of the structures, and excellent photographs, casts, and superb drawings (by Annie Hunter) of the Maya monuments at Copán and at several other major sites. A taste of the difficulties he encountered in the field can be had from the quotation which opens this chapter; some of the problems he faced with regard to the sculptures and casts which he brought back, equally if not more troublesome than his difficulties in Central America, can be gleaned from some of the recent writings of Ian Graham.[6]

Maudslay brought forth the results of his remarkable efforts in the five-volume *Biologia Centrali-Americana – Archaeology* (London, 1889–1902), which Sylvanus Morley referred to as 'the most important publication by which the science has been enriched'. Maudslay's massive work, and other monographs published by the Peabody Museum, finally made it possible for scholars interested in deciphering the inscribed hieroglyphs from the Classic period to work from reproductions of the monuments accurate enough to permit their intensive study. The Copán corpus of inscriptions became the subject of much scholarly work.

Besides recording and casting the free-standing stelae and altars at Copán, Maudslay also effected some preliminary excavations in several of the larger buildings. Although both García de Palacio and Stephens had written of 'walls', 'stairways', and 'mounds', and Stephens had even described several constructions as 'pyramids', neither had come to grips with the fact that

22 *John Owens of the Peabody Museum expedition (on muleback), taking plaster casts and molds to Puerto Barrios from Copán, by porter.*

masonry buildings stood atop the terraced platforms and pyramidal bases. Maudslay quickly realized this fact and set about investigating several of the more prominent buildings. He can be credited with the first detailed description of the Maya corbeled vault (or 'horizontal arch', in his terminology), and with discovering some of the most beautiful architectural sculpture ever found in the Maya area. Among the latter can be cited the inner chamber of Temple 22, the bench inside Temple 11, and the Hieroglyphic Stairway of Temple 26. Better yet, he excavated and made fairly extensive descriptions, drawings, and photographs of Temple 20, which the Copán River was to wash away in the decades to come: Maudslay's work represents virtually all that is known about this tall and apparently quite impressive structure. There are also notes or photographs or both of investigations executed in Structures 14, 16, and 24, and complete descriptions of all the stelae and altars which had been encountered up to then. Although he is rarely credited with it, it should also be recognized that Maudslay was the first individual to call attention to the great number of remains of stone houses and raised foundations found on either side of the Principal Group, 'evidence of the considerable population which must have at one time inhabited the plain'.[7]

Spurred on by Maudslay's work, Charles P. Bowditch, a great patron of Harvard's Peabody Museum of American Archaeology and Ethnology, and a devoted and accomplished decipherer of Maya hieroglyphics, obtained the rights to effect investigations in the ruins of Copán in 1891. Under the conditions of this agreement, the Peabody Museum secured the care of the antiquities of Honduras for a period of ten years, with the right to conduct excavations and permission to keep half of the objects found. There were four expeditions, undertaken in the years 1891–95 (the 1893–94 expedition being directed by Maudslay), during which a great deal of new digging and sculpture recording took place. The government of Honduras, after ousting the president who had signed this agreement, revoked it, and then reinstated it, but after 1895 it became impracticable for the work at Copán to be resumed.

Among the more important contributions of the Peabody Museum expeditions can be cited the discovery of nine previously unknown stelae (7, 8, 9, 11, 12, 13, 15, 16, and 19), excavations which uncovered the whole of the Hieroglyphic Stairway of Temple 26 (discovered but not dug out by Maudslay), and the uncovering of previously unknown inscriptions which graced the Reviewing Stand on the south side of Temple 11, and the interior bench of Temple 21a. The work on the Hieroglyphic Stairway was particularly significant, revealing as it did the longest inscribed text ever carved in the New World. This investigation was initiated by the director of the second expedition, John G. Owens, who unfortunately died of a tropical fever on 17 February 1893. (Sylvanus Morley, who had more than a few brushes with death in Maya lands himself, and Earl Morris, placed a headstone over Owen's grave in the Great Plaza, which reads 'J.G. Owens. Died April [sic] 1893. A Martyr to Science.') The work on the Stairway was completed in 1895 by

23 George B. Gordon of the Peabody Museum expedition, during work on the Hieroglyphic Stairway of Structure 10L 26.

George B. Gordon, who directed the fourth Peabody expedition, and wrote the monograph *The Hieroglyphic Stairway, Ruins of Copán.*[8]

Besides the discovery and documentation of sculpture, the members of the Peabody expeditions did a fair amount of excavation in and about the Principal Group for the purpose of acquiring specimens for the museum. In his 1920 book (see below), Morley succinctly assessed this aspect of their work: 'The excavations at Copán, particularly of the tombs, yielded a satisfactory return of objects.' Particularly noteworthy in this regard was the discovery of Tomb 1, which yielded numerous ceramic vessels and other objects, the most delicate and important of which was the inscribed peccary skull. To this day, the peccary skull stands as one of the finest works of Maya bone carving ever discovered. Another of the important achievements was Gordon's work in the Copán Valley. He produced the first topographic map of the valley, including the location of several monuments besides those found in the Principal Group. Gordon also directed excavations in a series of caves in the valley, uncovering the remains of the oldest inhabitants of the Copán valley yet encountered. For this discovery, the early ceramic complex represented in the caves and later found elsewhere in the valley was named in his honor.

The next important contribution to Copán archaeology was made by Herbert J. ('Joe') Spinden, who studied the stylistic development of the stelae

24 *The incised peccary skull from Tomb 1. The figures shown in the quatrefoil cartouche are shown on either side of an altar, with a stela in the background. Above the stela the short text carries the date 1 Ahau 8 Ch'en (placed at 8.17.0.0.0 in the Long Count, or* AD *376). On the sides of the skull can be seen a monkey, a jaguar, three running peccaries, and a deer.*

as part of his dissertation research at Harvard. Incorporated in the Peabody Memoir *A Study of Maya Art, its Subject-Matter and Historical Development*, the Copán material showed clearly that the stylistic development of Copán's art style could be used as an independent check on the veracity of the dating of the monuments from the Maya hieroglyphic texts. Frequently, the glyphs themselves were eroded and ambiguous, and in the case of Stela D, Spinden showed that the original 'decipherment' of the Long Count date had been out by nearly 200 years!

Although each of the individuals we have discussed up to this point made important, in some cases seminal, contributions, we must nonetheless acknowledge that the first individual really to realize that Copán was a city whose influence was felt as far away as Quiriguá in Guatemala was the indefatigable Maya archaeologist, explorer, and epigrapher, Sylvanus Griswold Morley. It was largely due to Morley's persuasive talents and unbounded energy that the Carnegie Institution became the largest single backer of Maya archaeology and ethnology during the first half of this century, a period referred to by George Stuart in his study of the history of Maya decipherment as the golden age of Maya archaeology.[9]

The Carnegie era

Copán was the first site which Morley investigated and wrote about extensively under Carnegie auspices. In 1920, Morley published a massive tome of some 644 pages entitled *The Inscriptions at Copán* (Carnegie Institution of Washington Publication 219), a study so thorough that it set the tone for all future epigraphic studies in the Maya area. This remarkable work is all the more impressive when one considers that it was the product of only ten weeks of actual investigations at the site, spread out over seven different visits from 1910 to 1919.

Morley's book was (and in some respects remains) the definitive catalog of the inscriptions, detailing the texts of every monument to which he had access, either through field observation or examination of other scholars' drawings and photographs. Morley arranged and analyzed the hieroglyphic texts chronologically, and concentrated above all on the dates and astronomical aspects of the texts, the primary interest of that time. Morley has been much criticized for attempting to fit all of the known Maya dates into the sequence of 'period endings' of 5, 10, 15, and 20-year intervals, both in his work at Copán and in his later researches throughout the Maya lowlands. Indeed, it is with great pride that he notes in the Copán book that his research into time reckoning tended 'to indicate that time in its different phases *may even have been the chief content of their inscriptions*' (emphasis in original).[10]

The belief that all the stone monuments were dedicated to mark the passage of time became so entrenched that it influenced scholars' views of the nature of ancient Maya society. Suddenly, all the dates must be associated with the movements of the heavenly bodies, or with the strict observance of the passage of time, or both; and the human figures represented must be calendar priests charged with making those observations (rather than the 'deified kings and heroes' of Stephens' writings). It soon became unquestioned dogma that ancient Maya society was a theocracy wherein scholarly priests, obsessed with observing the passage of time and the orderly movements of the heavenly bodies (and the gods that held sway over them), ruled over scattered hamlets of peaceful peasant farmers, who gathered occasionally in the great 'ceremonial centers' for observances of religious ritual. According to the conventional wisdom, Classic Maya society was so refined that no space was left in the inscriptions for such secular themes as warfare, accessions of rulers, or contacts and alliances between neighboring centers, let alone the vain claims of kings obsessed with their place in history. The clear references to warfare and sacrifice in the later art of Chichén Itzá were explained away as the result of the invasion of 'barbarous' peoples from Central Mexico. To the privileged Western scholars who studied them, the Classic Maya became idealized beyond any known culture on earth, perhaps owing to revulsion at the secular and vain (and very human) forces which produced two world wars. Without having done anything to bring it upon themselves, the Maya were thrust into an ivory tower.

To his credit, in his early writings, including the Copán book, Morley left the door open to other interpretations of the Classic-period inscriptions. In discussing the date which was most often repeated in the annals of the Copán inscriptions – 9.16.12.5.17 6 Caban 10 Mol (falling in our year AD 763) – Morley states that it was 'probably associated with some actual historical or astronomical event'. Recent research has shown that this event was in fact the accession to power of the 16th ruler of Copán, Yax Pac. He also noted that another date (our year AD 738), which did not fall on one of the period ending dates Morley so favored, was noted in the inscriptions of both Copán and Quiriguá. His surmise was that this fateful date 'is therefore probably to be regarded as the date of some actual historical happening . . . common to the history of both'. Little could he know that the date referred to would subsequently be proven to be the day on which the distinguished 13th ruler of Copán was beheaded by a rival from Quiriguá. Still, we must credit Morley with a larger vision than many of those who were to follow in his footsteps, for he made a point of noting that 'we may possibly look forward with some degree of confidence to finding . . . place-names, personal-names, and signs of generalized meaning, by the aid of which we will eventually be able to fill in the background of Maya history as successfully as we have already constructed its chronological framework.'[11]

In 1935 the Carnegie Institution, in collaboration with the government of Honduras, began a long-term project of investigations and restoration at the Principal Group of ruins. During the Carnegie years, numerous buildings and monuments were restored to the form that the visitor can see today: Ballcourt

25 *Structure 10L-11, view to the south. This was originally a two-storied building, and one of the most ornately adorned of all the architectural monuments of the Acropolis.*

A, Temple 11 (Structure 10L-11), Temple 22 (Structure 10L-22), the Hieroglyphic Stairway of Structure 10L-26, and the stelae of the Great Plaza. While Morley is to be credited with insuring that Copán was one of the archaeological sites selected for investigation by the Division of Historical Research, Gustav Stromsvik is to be credited with the directing and execution of the research and restoration work over the field seasons from 1935 to 1942, and a shorter stay in 1946. Stromsvik was a hearty, down-to-earth, and extremely practical man. In his tenure as Field Director, he re-erected the broken and fallen stelae; restored the ballcourt, the Hieroglyphic Stairway of Structure 10L-26 and the hieroglyphic panels of Temple 11; oversaw Aubrey Trik's restoration of Temple 22; built a huge protective stone dike to defend the Acropolis from the ravages of the river; rechanneled the river itself; and built the Copán Museum, and the fountain and park which still grace the central square of the village of Copán. Because of his energy and achievements, 'don Gustavo' remains something of a legend in Copán, even to this day.

Perhaps the most ambitious project undertaken by Stromsvik and his many colleagues was the restoration of the Hieroglyphic Stairway. After the city was

26 *Structure 10L-22, view to the northeast. Inside the 'monster mouth' doorway (note teeth flanking the entrance) can be seen some of the elaborate sculpture that embellishes the inner chamber of the structure.*

abandoned, the forces of nature toppled all but 30 steps of the stairway. Although the members of the first and third Peabody Museum expeditions had succeeded in uncovering all the blocks from the stairway inscription, they had merely laid them out in the open courtyard to the west of the stairway itself. In restoring these fallen sculptures, the idea was to conserve the individual blocks, rather than to leave them to the mercy of visitors and the vagaries of time and weather. At the same time, restoration of the stairway allowed the visitor a feeling for the original grandeur of the building itself.

Grandeur is perhaps the best adjective for the renderings of Copán produced by Tatiana Proskouriakoff. Having trained as an architect, Proskouriakoff became involved in making reconstruction drawings of the Maya ruins of Piedras Negras. Eventually, word of her drawings came to the attention of Morley, who arranged (with accustomed enthusiasm and fanfare) to have her travel to Copán and other sites in order to do more drawings for the Carnegie Institution. As part of the research for her reconstructions, Proskouriakoff did a number of studies of the façade sculptures from the various Copán temples. Among her keenest observations (made in her field notes) one can cite the identification of the macaw heads and wings with the ballcourt superstructure façades, the monster-mouth entrance on Temple 22, and the deduction that a huge crocodile originally adorned the exterior of Temple 11. She produced some truly remarkable reconstructions for her classic book *An Album of Maya Architecture* (Carnegie Institution of Washington, 1946).

Other important contributions made by the Carnegie team include the study and subsequent publication of the *Copán Ceramics* (1952), by John Longyear III, and the first detailed map of the ruins visible on the surface in the valley, published as the frontispiece to Longyear's book. Longyear's reconstruction of the valley's history borrows heavily from the model developed by Morley, positing the invasion of Maya speakers and establishment of the stela cult in the 5th century AD, and ending with only a small and insignificant Postclassic population after the stone monuments ceased to be erected. Longyear's study, however, benefited from the many observations he was able to make from the purely archaeological research that had by that point been conducted at Copán. For example, it was now clear that there was an 'Archaic', pre-inscription (or pre-Maya, in their view) population in the valley, and that there was evidence for a post-monument (Postclassic) occupation, as well.

Longyear and Stromsvik had been aided in their sorting and study of the ceramics and other artifacts that were cataloged and placed in the Copán Museum by Jesús Núñez Chinchilla, a Copanec who went on to become a physician, and eventually the first Director of the Instituto Hondureño de Antropología e Historia (IHAH). As Director of the IHAH, Dr Núñez continued some of the unfinished restoration work in the Principal Group, but did most of his excavation work in the valley. Núñez dug a fascinating offertory cache in a cave on the south side of the valley, which was filled with jadeites of virtually every size and description; and excavated a large residential compound just north of the Great Plaza, which proved to have a very long sequence of occupation and graves.

Recent investigations

In the mid-1970s, Gordon R. Willey, Bowditch Professor of Central American Archaeology and Ethnology at Harvard University, was invited by the then Director of the IHAH, Dr José Adán Cueva (another Copanec), to come to Copán to design a long-term program of research and restoration, to be sponsored by the Honduran government. In consultation with Robert J. Sharer and William R. Coe of the University Museum of the University of Pennsylvania, Willey made a survey of the archaeology of the Principal Group and of the Copán Valley, including the four pockets of valley bottomlands upstream from the Copán pocket. The results of their survey, and their recommendations for further work, were published in the journal of the IHAH, *Yaxkin*. Willey then set about to get the larger project started, having procured funding from the National Science Foundation and the Bowditch Fund for mapping and excavations in the valley.

Willey initiated a modern, multi-disciplinary approach at Copán: the Peabody Museum Copán Sustaining Area Project. He sought to understand the public monuments within their larger social and economic contexts, to reconstruct Maya society from the bottom up. To do this, Willey brought in a cultural geographer, a river geomorphologist and pedologist, a geologist, and several botanists to reconstruct the ancient environment and agricultural history of the Copán region, while he and his students (the author among them) reconstructed the ancient settlement patterns through site survey, transit mapping, and excavation. In three seasons of work (1975–77), great strides were made in all these areas, but circumstances prevented Willey from being able to accept the offer of becoming the Director of the Honduran-sponsored project. Nevertheless, his methods of mapping, his ceramic typology, and the horizontal exposure of residential architecture he pioneered, served as the baseline for the continuing study of Copán Valley archaeology. Furthermore, his multi-disciplinary, holistic approach serves as an inspiration for all present and future scholars.

The concern with hieroglyphic and iconographic analysis of the Copán monuments was reflected in two books published in the 1970s: Francis Robicsek's *Copán: Home of the Mayan Gods* (1971), and Joyce Marcus' *Emblem and State in the Classic Maya Lowlands* (1976). Robicsek's book was a well-illustrated synthesis of the work effected at Copán up to that date. Containing many insights into the size and nature of the Copán kingdom and its historical development, *Emblem and State* was a more extensive and ambitious undertaking that synthesized epigraphic studies from the entire southern Maya lowlands. By combining Central Place Theory with Berlin's definition of emblem-glyphs, Marcus proposed a model in which Tikal was one of four major centers controlling the southern lowlands in AD 731. She derived this date from the dedication of Copán Stela A, whose hieroglyphic text cites Copán, Tikal, Calakmul(?), and Palenque in association with the glyphs representing the four cardinal directions and statements indicating that these were the 'four [cities] on high'. These four kingdoms were seen as primary centers, which ruled secondary centers, tertiary centers, and villages.

Beginning in late 1977, the first phase of the Honduran government-sponsored Proyecto Arqueologico Copán (PAC I) was initiated, under the direction of Claude F. Baudez of the French Centre de Recherche Scientifique. During Baudez' tenure, important new insights were obtained from the completion, under the author's direction, of the map of the valley settlements, by the excavation of numerous test-pits and trenches in both the valley and the Principal Group, through continuing ecological studies, and by renewed studies of the monumental art and inscriptions. With becoming modesty and astute anticipation, Baudez decided to call the three dense volumes of primary research produced by his project simply the *Introducción a la Arqueología de Copán, Honduras* (Tegucigalpa, 1983).

William T. Sanders of Pennsylvania State University was invited by Adán

Cueva in 1980 to direct the second phase (PAC II, 1980–85). Sanders' research design addressed a number of problems first posed by Willey, continued to pursue important processes documented by Baudez in PAC I, and considered several new problems. The overarching goal was to reconstruct the population and land-use history of the entire Copán drainage basin. This baseline would serve as the foundation from which the economic and political evolution of the Copán city-state could be described and explained, after an intensive study of the function and organization of buildings occupied by all strata of society (including the royal family) and the analysis of the monumental inscriptions, art, and architecture of the Principal Group.

Not satisfied with the limited coverage of the regional settlement system achieved by the previous surveys (which concentrated heavily on the Copán pocket), Sanders and his Project Co-Director, David Webster (also of Pennsylvania State University), extended the survey to an area eventually covering 135 sq. km. Field mapping and subsequent excavations were undertaken to determine the size and history of settlement and land-use in the whole region of the Copán and immediately adjacent drainage systems, and to obtain a clear vision of regional cultural geography.

At the same time, numerous wide-exposure excavations were undertaken in the residential area to the east of the Principal Group, following the methodology developed by Willey. These excavations were carried out to test a series of propositions about social ranking and economic organization in the urban sector of Copán where Willey and Richard Leventhal (one of his students) had defined four levels of settlements, thought to represent different socio-economic levels within ancient Copán society.[12] The excavations in the Sepulturas area were extremely informative, and full of surprises. The buildings were also subsequently restored by Carlos Rudy Larios Villalta, making a fine addition to the Copán archaeological park. (Indeed, Copán is the only Classic-period site where residential architecture is so well restored and available to the public, fitting testimony to Willey's and Sanders' methods and research interests.)

The surveys and excavations were to be supplemented by specific research projects undertaken by Sanders' students. These included studies of the human skeletal remains to analyze ancient demography, nutrition, and disease; pollen recovery and analysis to reconstruct vegetational and agricultural history; an analysis of the labor input involved in construction; a study of soils and soil use; a study of ground stone manufacture and use; the function of structures based on structure size, layout, and associated features and artifacts; an analysis of ethnicity based on the excavation of an anomolous and possibly foreign or foreign-derived enclave attached to one of the larger residential compounds; a study of domestic activities at the various buildings of the residential area; an analysis of lithic workshop debris, and lithic use and discard patterns in the valley; and the dating of the valley settlements and the process of the 'collapse'.[13] Sanders himself conducted a study of modern land-

27 *Group 9N-8, a Type 4 residential site in Las Sepulturas, as restored by Rudy Larios during PAC II. The patriarch of the élite family that lived here resided in the large, elaborate building in the background (Structure 9N-82). Although presently covered by a thatched roof to protect the hieroglyphic bench inside, this structure was constructed entirely of masonry in its original state, with other sculptures adorning the now collapsed upper portion (see ill. 27).*

use patterns, cropping patterns and yields per hectare, and residential architecture. These important studies have taken Copán archaeology far beyond what has been possible previously at any other Maya site.

Professional colleagues from PAC I were also invited to participate in Sanders' project. Claude Baudez continued his research on the iconography of the Copán monuments, supervising the documentation of the sculptures by the project photographer and artists. His colleague Berthold Riese continued his epigraphic survey and documentation project. Rene Viel continued as Project Ceramicist, and completed a study of the ceramic sequence of the Copán pocket. The author also joined Sanders' project, and continued to direct

28 *(Opposite) The west figure of the entablature on the north façade of Structure 9N-82, reconstructed in a large sandbox made for the purpose of refitting the fallen mosaic sculpture fragments. The figure sits on a sign that is used in the writing system, and reads* na, *or 'house'.*

excavations begun with PAC I at Group 9N-8, which had been found to contain the longest occupation history in the valley, and later took on the reconstruction of the site's mosaic façades.

Perhaps the most exciting excavation of Sanders' project was that of Patio A of Group 9N-8, the largest residential compound investigated. During the first month of excavation, David Webster and Elliot Abrams uncovered an exquisite hieroglyphic bench (or throne) in Structure 9N-82, dating to the reign of the last ruler of Copán.[14] Webster and Abrams excavated three sides of Structure 9N-82 in 1980–81, and the author excavated the fourth in 1982. Based on the carefully-recorded positions of the fallen fragments, it was possible to reconstruct how the mosaic sculptures had fallen from their original positions on all four sides of the building. Re-articulation of the sculpture carried out by Barbara Fash and the author, and a reconstruction drawing done in collaboration with Rudy Larios, convinced us all that it was indeed possible to reconstruct (at least hypothetically) the form and content of Copán mosaic sculpture façades.

Thus, an unforeseen development of Sanders' project was the formation of the Copán Mosaics Project in 1985. This initial work to reconstruct one building's mosaic façades spawned an intense effort to achieve systematic scientific investigation and reconstruction of the façades of numerous buildings in the valley, as well as others in the Principal Group of ruins. Our experiences at the 'House of the Bacabs', as Structure 9N-82 is known, underscored the need for conservation of the long-neglected and often badly-deteriorating sculpture fragments scattered about the Principal Group.

The goals of the project are to conserve, document, re-articulate, analyze, reconstruct, and interpret the tens of thousands of fragments of tenoned mosaic façade sculptures which originally adorned dozens of Late Classic masonry structures in the Copán Valley. The research focus is on the use of ideology by the royal court to define and protect its power, to achieve consensus, and to govern the supporting population of the kingdom through time. The project is therefore particularly interested in the first evidence of public art and associated ritual, the monuments accompanying the consolidation of a regional political base in the 5th century AD, and the responses to a series of political and eventually economic setbacks precipitating the collapse of the Copán state. However, before getting too involved with the 'big picture', it is equally important to deal with the immense task of reconstructing Copán's temples. Methods devised for doing this have proven productive, and the Copán Mosaics Project has been expanded in scope. It is presently incorporated in the Honduran government-sponsored Copán Acropolis Archaeological Project, directed by the author.

The great challenge for present and future Mayanists at Copán and elsewhere is to interpret the public monuments and their often explicit political and religious themes within the larger social and economic contexts which framed the growth and decline of the various Classic period kingdoms.

CHAPTER FOUR

FROM PRECLASSIC TO CLASSIC IN THE COPÁN VALLEY

The Preclassic period in Mesoamerica

In Mesoamerica, the Preclassic period (*c.* 2000 BC–AD 250) was initially defined as the time span of those cultures which preceded the elaboration of the great Classic-period civilizations, including the Classic Maya. In fact, research has shown that the Preclassic period was the most important time period in the evolution of Mesoamerican civilization. This point has been demonstrated in much recent literature on the Olmecs and their contemporaries in Mesoamerica, including David Grove's book, *Chalcatzingo* (1984), in the present series. During the Preclassic all the basic adaptations for civilized, urban life evolved in Mesoamerica: intensive agriculture adapted to various ecological settings; extensive networks of interaction and exchange; hierarchical organization of power, and for the distribution of goods and information; nucleation of the supporting population around central places ('ceremonial' or 'organizational centers'); and the ideological adaptations necessary to sustain institutionalized kingship as the linchpin of the entire cultural system. For this reason, many prefer to use the term 'Formative' to refer to this period.

The search for the Copán Preclassic

Research at Copán has included a program of test-pit excavations, and since 1976 over 1000 pits have been dug. The analysis to date suggests that the valley's initial occupation by sedentary farmers took place in the latter half of the second millennium BC, climaxing with a densely-nucleated population from the 7th to 10th centuries AD, and eventually ending with its virtual abandonment, perhaps as late as AD 1200. Much of the information on the Preclassic period presented here is derived from the investigations carried out by the author on Group 9N-8 in 1978, 1981, and 1983.

In attempting to find evidence of the history of habitation and land-use in the valley, the test-pitting program of PAC I employed a variety of different sampling methods. The goal was to produce unbiased information which would accurately reflect the presence and relative density of human occupation and the land-use of the valley's varied physiographic zones through time.

To fulfill this goal we used random systematic stratified unaligned sampling, employing two different area or 'grain' sizes. That is, we selected the areas for investigation from a gridded map of the different physiographic zones:

floodplain; low river terrace; high river terrace and foothills; upper slopes. After deciding what proportion of the total surface of each physiographic zone we wanted to investigate, we selected the actual areas using random numbers that were not allowed to bunch up or align in a way that might unfavorably bias the results. The two different grain sizes for investigation consisted of a 52 × 52m unit (for zones with a strong likelihood or actual evidence of heavy use) and 500 × 500 m areas (for steep and sloping areas with less likelihood or evidence of intensive use). The random sampling, we soon realized, would give us objective measures, but would also compel us to leave uninvestigated a series of localities that had all the appearances of having had a long and possibly continuous occupation sequence, namely the very large architectural compounds (known as 'Types 3 and 4'). On this premise we supplemented our random samples with purposive, biased samples of the large architectural compounds in the valley, in order to get as complete a picture of the occupation history as our time and resources would allow.[1]

The picture that emerged was that the earliest occupants of the Copán Valley established themselves on the fertile alluvium at the bottom of the Copán pocket, where they practiced subsistence agriculture and lived in predominantly perishable housing. Although present indications are that most of the population lived on the alluvial bottomlands, early ceramics were found in the foothills zones as well, indicating that this zone was also used and possibly settled, though in a less intensive or dense fashion. A number of interesting and long-lived features have been found dating to the Middle Preclassic (known as the 'Uir ceramic phase' at Copán – 900–400 BC) in the valley bottomlands. Nevertheless, with the exception of the cave where Gordon found evidence for the burial of several individuals during the Middle Preclassic (see below), no remains indicating large-scale, sustained or intensive Middle Preclassic use of the foothills zone, let alone of the upper slopes, have yet been uncovered.

It was during the process of uncovering one important Middle Preclassic feature in the bottomlands that evidence of another, still earlier occupation was encountered. In 1978, we decided to excavate test-pits in the plaza areas of one of the very largest architectural compounds 600 m east of the Principal Group. (Originally labelled CV 36 by Willey and Leventhal this compound is now known as Group 9N-8.[2]) This site consists of 50 structures grouped around 11 courtyards, with some structures nearly 5 m high in their unexcavated states. The number and sizes of the mounds, and the fact that the largest ones in the center of the site sat atop a large, artificial platform, led us to infer that this site should contain evidence of a long occupation history. Our efforts were rewarded in a test-probe dug in the center of 'Patio A', the open courtyard shared by the most imposing set of buildings at this site.

Two meters below the courtyard surface, a set of human burials was uncovered, two of which had Middle Preclassic ceramics very similar to those discovered by Gordon in the Copán caves in 1893. The incised and painted

29 Aerial photograph taken in 1978 looking east at the eastern limit of the Sepulturas area (foreground), and the bottomlands east and south of the Copán River. The larger mounds of Group 9N-8 are visible in the foreground, with the author's original test excavation in Patio A visible in the center of the open area bounded by the four highest mounds.

designs on one of the vessels carried the 'flame eyebrow' motif so common to the Early and Middle Preclassic ceramics, and associated with the first stirrings of complex religion and society in Mesoamerica. It became obvious that the burials extended in all directions, showing that the feature was a large one. Above the burial ground was a sequence of Early, Middle, and Late Classic cobble constructions and floors, indicating that the occupation sequence at the site was indeed a long and complete one. What we could not know at the time was that some 10 m away lay the remains of a still earlier occupation. When we began the large-scale stripping of the plaza in 1981, and extended the investigation of the burial area to the north, we uncovered the earliest house yet encountered in Copán.

The Early Preclassic period (known as the 'Rayo ceramic phase' – 1300–900 BC) house was discovered at the south end of the patio, 4 m below the surface. It comprised an area roughly 2.5 × 4 m, rectangular with rounded corners, and easily distinguished from the surrounding sterile soil by the amount of carbon, burned earth, organic debris, and artifacts found within its confines. The carbon and burned earth showed that many hearth fires had burned in this house. A carbon sample from the house has been assigned a calibrated date of

30 The extensive excavations of Patio A, Group 9N-8, looking south. Structure 9N-82 and its hieroglyphic bench are seen at the top of the photograph; the central trench that revealed the earliest occupations is shown here at the level of sterile soil.

1390 ± 60 BC. This structure would seem to have been used for all the domestic activities of the day, and among the discarded artifacts found were fragments of grinding stones (for preparing maize flour), a variety of ceramic cooking and serving vessels, flint and obsidian tools for cutting and scraping, bones of edible mammals, and figurines which could have served either as children's toys or as sacred objects. Excavations in other parts of Patio A were also taken to the same level, without finding any traces of other contemporary structures or activity areas. Until such time as the whole of Patio A can be excavated to sterile soil, we can only conjecture as to whether this early structure stood alone or in the company of others.

The ceramics, as analyzed by Rene Viel, indicate strong interaction with the Pacific coast and highlands to the south and west of Copán, in adjacent El Salvador, Guatemala, and even Chiapas, Mexico. Viel's opinion is that these earliest occupants of the valley derived from ancestral highland or coastal populations which were probably Maya-speaking. Other scholars interpret the Veracruz-Tabasco Olmec populations, and those of the adjacent sectors of Chiapas and southern Guatemala during the Early and Middle Preclassic periods, as Mixe-Zoque speakers, and this possibility must also be considered. In any case, the earliest Copanecs were certainly not the same population found in the earliest hamlets in the central or 'core' area of the southern Maya lowlands, at sites such as Tikal, Uaxactun, Seibal, or even the ancient remains discovered at Cuello in Belize. From the beginning, Copán was geographically, economically, and to a certain degree culturally, distinct from other Maya lowlands sites, having many features which are more highland than lowland.

After this Early Preclassic house was abandoned, the site itself was apparently also abandoned, because 50 cm of silt were laid over it by the river; and no artifacts were found in this silt. (The wonder, frankly, is that the fragile remains of this perishable house were not washed away. And one shudders to think how many others on the alluvial plain may have suffered such a fate, at various points in the valley's history.)

The 'Olmec horizon' materials from Group 9N-8

Many generations later, the first stone architecture for which we have evidence at Copán was built above and to one side of where the Early Preclassic house had stood. This was a cobblestone platform measuring some 6 m east–west × 13 m north–south; only two courses – 35 cm – of its height remained. At a slightly later date, another platform, of similar dimensions, was built just to the north of the first one. The platforms may have stood higher in their original state, and probably supported perishable structures on top. Unfortunately, subsequent constructions by the Early Classic inhabitants of the site razed the upper parts of both of the Middle Preclassic platforms. Nonetheless, preservation of the lower parts has enabled us to arrive at some fairly solid conclusions on the dating and use of these buildings.

A series of sub-floor burials were found in both platforms, with Uir phase (900–400 BC) ceramics identical to those found by Gordon in the cave burials. The unusual bottle forms and elaborately incised funerary vessels are considered to be a specialized 'sub-complex' of the Uir phase ceramics that apparently were used only in burials. This sub-complex was named after its initial discoverer, George B. Gordon. The burials were all found at an elevation slightly below the second course of the cobblestones which formed the outer facing of the two platforms. Sub-floor burials were the most common form of disposing of the dead in Mesoamerica, and the mere presence of these graves implies that the stone platforms served as residences for the people who were buried there. Some of the uppermost burials had obviously been much disturbed, either by redeposition or by secondary burials, and we are faced with the possibility that the Early Classic peoples, in removing the upper half of the platforms, may have disturbed the human remains reposing there. In other cases it appears that the Middle Preclassic occupants themselves pushed aside the bones of earlier burials to accommodate new ones. In any case, the remains of 15 individuals were found in the south platform, and at least 32 individuals in the north platform. Unfortunately, the silt which served as the fill for the platforms was highly acidic, and the state of preservation of the bones was poor, making studies of age, sex, and demography very difficult.

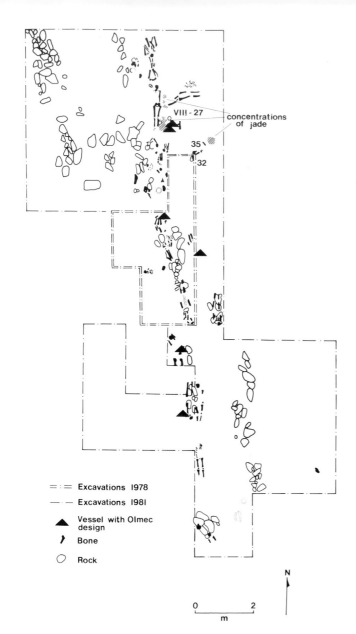

31 (Left) *Plan of the Gordon sub-complex cobblestone platforms and sub-floor burials from Patio A, Group 9N-8. The location of Burial VIII-27 in the north platform is shown.*

32 (Above) *A fluted bottle from the Gordon sub-complex burials at Group 9N-8. Such bottle forms are a prominent feature of many Early and Middle Preclassic ceramic assemblages in Mesoamerica. Height 20 cm.*

There are intriguing differences in the burial patterns found at the two Gordon sub-complex platforms. In the south platform, stone cists were used to line the graves, and in one case stone capstones were laid over the body after it was placed in the grave. In the north platform, some stones were found in association with one secondary burial, but otherwise no evidence of cists or capstones was found. On the other hand, jade offerings were unearthed with several burials in the north platform (in one case comprising over 300 drilled beads and jaguar claw effigies), but were found with only one individual in the south platform. Ceramics with complex incised religious imagery, however,

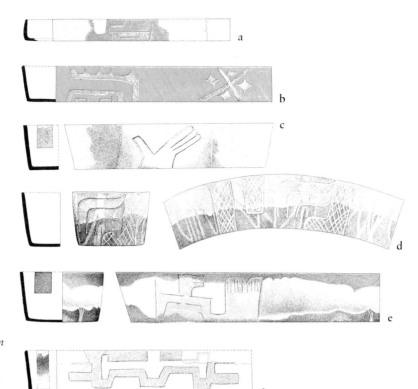

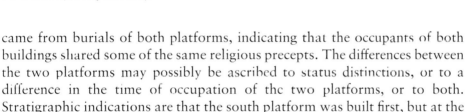

*33 Incised ceramics of the Gordon sub-complex burials from Group 9N-8: **a** and **b** 'flame-eyebrow' motif; **c** and **d** 'hand-wing' motif; **e** shark motif; **f** serpent motif.*

came from burials of both platforms, indicating that the occupants of both buildings shared some of the same religious precepts. The differences between the two platforms may possibly be ascribed to status distinctions, or to a difference in the time of occupation of the two platforms, or to both. Stratigraphic indications are that the south platform was built first, but at the present time we have no secure way of assessing how much time elapsed between its construction and that of the north platform.

The ceramics with incised designs and the jade offerings associated with these early burials are of great interest to specialists in Preclassic Mesoamerica. Both David Grove and Michael Coe have suggested that these may be the earliest finely worked jadeites yet discovered in the New World. The ceramics from the graves are even more intriguing, containing as they do the artistic expressions of the earliest complex culture to develop in this isolated valley, far from the Olmec 'heartland' of coastal Veracruz and Tabasco, Mexico. The designs include the crocodile deity with 'flame eyebrow', the 'hand-wing' motif (in two variants), and what Grove identifies as a shark. The hand-wing and shark images were also represented on two of the vessels discovered by Gordon in the Copán caves.[3]

One interpretation of these religious images is that they represent lineage patrons. In the Valley of Oaxaca, for example, the flame eyebrow motif is found almost exclusively with the human remains in certain areas, while the paw-wing motif is found almost exclusively with the burials of the remaining sites.[4] The explanation may be that there were lineage groups whose patrons were immutable, and that images of those patrons were carved on the vessels placed in the graves of their revered dead. This explanation is a fascinating one, and may be applicable to the Copán stone platforms as well, for it turns out that the vessels with flame-eyebrow images are confined to the north platform, whereas those with the hand-wing designs are found only in the south platform. Were the two platforms the respective residences of two lineages who intermarried, with the ceramics serving as both lineage badges and attestations of religious fealty? Though this is a compelling explanation of the observed patterns, we must always leave the door open to alternative explanations, especially to the possibility that the differences may be the result of time, given that one platform's construction pre-dates that of the other.

The jade and ceramic offerings associated with Burial VIII-27 of the north platform represent an offering of unprecedented wealth in the Maya area at this early date. Four ceramic vessels, nine polished stone celts, and over 300 drilled jade objects were placed in this grave. The amount of work represented by so many highly-polished jades is astonishing. Jade is harder than steel, and the only tools the ancient Mesoamericans had to cut, shape, and above all, sand and polish it were twine, stone drills, and sand and water. The jaguar claw effigies are also exquisitely worked, and the whole of the offering is highly impressive. (Today it forms the centerpiece of the Preclassic case in the Copán Museum.)

But, as with many archaeological finds, there is much about this grave that is not understood. Next to the offering were a decapitated skeleton on one side, and the long bone of another individual on the other. Underneath the jades were two children's skulls. This rich offering may have been a ritual sacrifice and burial of sacred objects, or it may have been burial furniture to accompany an honored member of society into the afterlife, whose grave was subsequently disturbed when burying other individuals.

In any case, the presence of such offerings, and the complex set of religious beliefs and icons represented in the incised ceramics, indicates a level of social and economic organization above that of simple peasant agriculturalists. Did the early inhabitants of the valley establish themselves on an artery of communication with Olmec traders, or with Pacific or highland Guatemalan chiefs and entrepreneurs? At this point we can only speculate on the reasons why complex culture became established here. More vexsome still is the question of why the society represented in the Gordon sub-complex did not evolve an even more complex and inclusive socio-economic system quickly and directly. This, after all, is what we would expect, given the perfectly 'circumscribed' environment represented by the Copán Valley, and the clear evidence for contact and exchange with outside forces. But that is not what the archaeological record indicates to have happened.

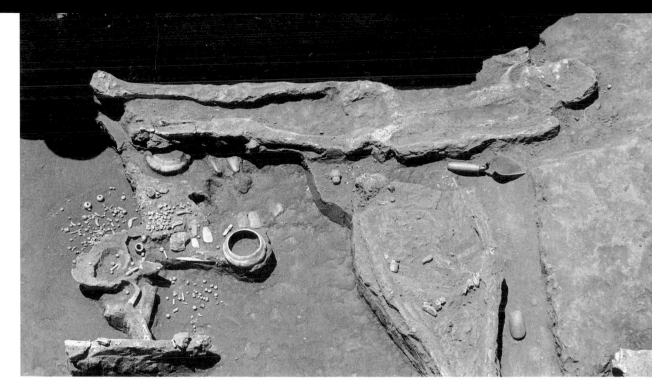

34 *Gordon sub-complex burials from Patio A, Group 9N-8. Burial VIII-27, with its concentration of jade beads, celts, and jaguar effigy claws, appears at the left.*

The Late Preclassic to Classic

Other than the cave burials and Group 9N-8, only one of the more than 1000 test pits in the valley has revealed Gordon sub-complex ceramics. And no other Middle Preclassic (Uir ceramic phase) or Late Preclassic (known as the 'Chabij' ceramic phase, 400 BC – AD 100) burials have been discovered. There is ample possibility that the size and distribution of our samples has missed important settlements, particularly in the case of the poorly-documented remains buried under the modern village of Copán. Even so, the pattern revealed by our tests thus far is consistent in all parts of the valley. After the establishment of several settlements in the valley bottomlands, and use of the land (if not permanent settlement) in the foothills zones of the valley during the Middle Preclassic period, there seems to have been either a population reduction or a tight nucleation of settlement during the Late Preclassic.

There was clearly a Late Preclassic settlement in the area south and west of the Acropolis, and our excavations underneath the Acropolis may yet uncover more evidence that it extended to that area as well. There are hints of Late Preclassic occupation in the area covered by the village, but nothing to suggest a large and well-organized population. The Copán situation represents an anomaly, since the Late Preclassic was a boom time in most of the Maya area, and in non-Maya lands to the south and east as well. Impressive works of art and architecture signal the emergence of complex society in many parts of the highlands of Guatemala (notably at the site of Kaminaljuyu), in the Pacific foothills (at Abaj Takalik and El Baúl), in western El Salvador (at Chalchuapa and Santa Leticia), in non-Maya central Honduras (at Yarumela and Los Naranjos), and certainly in the southern Maya lowlands, where such sites as El Mirador, Nakbé, Uaxactun, Cerros, Lamanai, Kohunlich, and others boast large monumental architecture with complex religious imagery in stucco.

Why Copán seems to have stayed at a simple level of organization at this point is an open and unresolved question. Circumscription theory would predict that the small confines of the valley and the constricted nature of the best agricultural land would make it the ideal setting for the emergence of complex culture by the Late Preclassic period, particularly given the evidence for the development of complex religion and social ranking provided by the Middle Preclassic burials. Likewise, the 'interaction sphere model' – which posits that contact between societies on an equal level of socio-cultural development promotes the evolution of more hierarchical institutions and the material trappings of complex culture – would also predict that Copán should have participated in the exciting developments taking place at other nascent centers to the east, south, west, and northwest. This anomaly points out the need to be flexible in the application of theoretical models, and cautious about our ability to predict the course of human history, even when 'necessary conditions' of a particular theory or set of theories have been met.

Beginning *c.* AD 100, another ceramic phase, known as 'Bijac', is recognized for the Copán Valley. It is characterized by the continuation of the Usulutan ceramics so abundant in the Chabij phase, but now in the form of tetrapod bowls with mammiform supports. A large number of other vessel types and pastes appear, including the very earliest polychrome pottery. Comparative ceramic studies indicate that Copán's commercial ties continued with the highland and foothills zones to the south and west, but not with the Maya lowlands to the northwest, showing once again that Copán was geographically and culturally distinct from its counterparts in the Maya lowlands. But its population seems to have been on the upswing, for Bijac phase ceramics were found in test-pits in more than one physiographic zone in the valley, and in fair quantities in the alluvial bottomlands in the area of the Principal Group. In the Bijac phase, we once again find evidence for permanent, stone constructions, this time at several different locations.

At Group 9N-8, Bijac phase peoples constructed another very large cobblestone platform, which extended some 50 m north–south by 12 m east–west. This platform was built directly on top of the Middle Preclassic platforms, and its builders possibly removed the upper half of the earlier constructions for fill and facing stones. The Bijac platform was expanded at a later date by the addition of a new façade of cobblestones on the outside of the east face, separated from the original façade by a meter of red silt fill, increasing the height of the platform by some 40 cm. Two sub-floor burials accompanied by Bijac phase ceramic vessels were found inside this building: an adult in the earlier platform, and a child in the later one. Scattered Bijac phase sherds were

35 The two façades of the Bijac phase cobblestone platforms uncovered in Patio A of Group 9N-8 (view to the north–northwest). A building wall atop the final-phase platform extends over the exterior face of the earlier façade platform.

found in the fill, leaving no question as to the time of construction, as well as the occupation, of both platforms. A cobblestone masonry wall pertaining to a building constructed atop the platform was fortunately preserved when the Bijac platforms were themselves buried at a later date, and is evidence that in addition to stone platforms, the Group 9N-8 Bijac peoples also had stone rather than perishable walls in their superstructures. The ceramics found with the two graves indicate a concern for the afterlife, as well as access to finely crafted wares: an exquisite basal-flanged polychrome bowl was placed with the adult; and with the child were three small but delicately rendered pots. However, no jade was found with either burial, and we should not consider these to have been high-status individuals.

In his investigations of the remains buried beneath the Great Plaza in the Principal Group, Charles Cheek uncovered four construction phases dating to the final century of the Bijac ceramic phase. The size, layout, plaster floors, dressed stone masonry, and offerings associated with these structures indicate that their occupants were of a much higher social standing than their contemporaries in Group 9N-8.[5] Similarly, plastered, dressed-stone masonry Bijac phase buildings found 200 m to the west of the Great Plaza in excavation Operation IV/123 show that others in the immediate vicinity of what even then may have been the Principal Group, were also better off than the relatively more distant and less pretentious occupants of Group 9N-8.

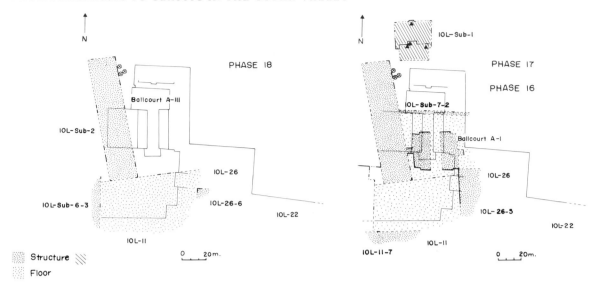

Structure
Floor
⊗ Burial
▲ Cache

36 Plans of the Great Plaza/Hieroglyphic Stairway Plaza area of the Principal Group during Cheek's construction stages 16–18 (at the end of the Bijac phase, c.AD 400).

Offerings found with Structure 10L-sub 2 in the Great Plaza included a black human effigy pot virtually identical to examples found at Kaminaljuyu, showing the continued closeness of links with the Guatemala highlands. This structure measures 85 m north–south by 18 m east–west, and is larger than anything else found in the valley at this time. Two other nearby buildings, one buried under Structure 10L-26 and the other under Structure 10L-6, were contemporaneous with Structure 10L-sub-2 during Cheek's Phase 18, and apparently formed the nucleus of what was to become the Principal Group. Shortly thereafter, the first ballcourt was constructed, indicating that ceremonialism was becoming a prime concern of the nascent Copán élites. By the end of Cheek's Phase 15 (*c.* AD 400), there were a minimum of seven buildings in the Great Plaza/Hieroglyphic Stairway Plaza sector of the Principal Group. Robert Sharer's investigations of the Archaeological Cut and his tunneling operations in the East Court indicate that there were some monumental constructions in this sector of the Acropolis dating to the same time, as well.

At present, no hieroglyphic inscriptions carved during the late Bijac phase are known. However, we should note that two 'pot-belly' sculptures of Chabij or Bijac phase manufacture were found buried underneath Copán Stelae 4 and 5 (erected in the Late Classic), indicating that sculpture carving did take place at Copán in the Late Preclassic or Early Classic. And inscriptions on Stelae 4 and I cite an event which occurred in AD 159 that may have to do with the founding of Copán as a kingdom. In any case, the archaeological record does indicate that the population was growing and that certain segments of it were beginning to separate themselves socially from their contemporaries.

The Middle Classic

It is during the succeeding, Middle Classic period (known as the 'Acbi ceramic phase' at Copán – AD 400–700), that truly significant changes in society took place in the Copán Valley. Not coincidentally, it was during this time that the valley population underwent a notable growth in size and distribution across the landscape. All of our test-pit excavations affirmed this, as did the extensive stratigraphic excavations at Group 9N-8 and at the Principal Group. The number of excavation units recovering ceramics, features, construction, and burials literally doubles from Bijac to Acbi times.

Most of the population seems to have preferred to settle in the bottomlands on either side of the Principal Group. In order to accommodate so many people in such a small area, the society had to make certain changes, changes that would enable the smooth transfer of information, goods, and services to the individuals at the top of the system. Indeed, it was those very same individuals who strove to promote nucleation, diversification of goods and services, and the creation of a power hierarchy in the first place. This has always been the nature of socio-economic 'evolution' in all corners of the globe. Whether motivated by competition, or by perceived benefits of unification, or both, human societies the world over develop institutions whose central goal is the amassing and maintenance of power in all forms.

No society in the history of humankind has made dramatic and lasting social changes without the benefit of a set of ideas or beliefs which would justify and legitimize, if not blatantly demand, the transformations that were to occur. Ideology has in many documented cases been the driving force behind expansionist states. For the ancient Maya, local élites began to rise above their contemporaries through the formulation and skillful implementation of a religious ideology which reified their privileged positions in cosmological terms. Evidence for the latter comes in the form of the nature and distribution of the earliest public displays of religious art. Rather than the obsession with portraiture and individual history manifest in the free-standing Classic-period monuments, the earliest known (Late Preclassic) religious art in the Maya lowlands comprises images of deities adorning large pyramidal buildings. The structures themselves, and the images which adorn them, place the rulers of the society in a larger supernatural context from which they perform rites and duties for the benefit of the people who sustained them in those positions. In the words of Linda Schele and David Freidel, the earliest Maya temples and their art were 'stage fronts' for the performance of important public rituals, the purpose of which was to forge coherence in society and legitimize the exalted status of the men who shouldered the burdens (and privileges) of office.[6] It was not until several centuries later that the emphasis of public art shifted from the sacred context (the building in which ritual was performed by the ruler) to the individual who filled the office (portraits of the rulers themselves).

It has traditionally been held that the population inhabiting the Copán

Valley did not become 'Maya' until the introduction of the stela cult and associated hieroglyphic writing system in the early part of the 5th century AD. What was until recently the first securely dated Long Count date (9.2.10.0.0, or AD 485) on Stela 24 was thought by scholars such as Morley and Longyear to signal the time when Maya élites from the Petén area of the southern lowlands invaded the valley and established themselves as rulers of the local, non-Maya populace. This model posited the wholesale importation of Classic Maya civilization, by then developed to the point of the personality cult manifested by the inscribed stelae. However, the evidence of our new investigations in the valley and the excavation of the earlier public architecture in the Great Plaza have forced us to revise this view. Rather than seeing lowland Maya civilization as borrowed by Copán on or about AD 485, it would be more reasonable to conclude that it developed locally, and at an earlier date.[7]

Beginning at the end of the Bijac phase and continuing into the Acbi phase – i.e. during the years *c.* AD 300–450 – the dominant members of Copán society began constructing buildings in a regional variant of the Maya style. As time passed, their prestige and external connections grew, and they became able to produce inscribed monuments of their own, perhaps as much as a century after their first large-scale public architecture was built. Present indications are that the people who built these monuments were the descendants of those who had inhabited the Copán pocket for over a millennium, and that their strongest trade connections continued to be with both the highlands and Pacific foothills of Guatemala, and with the non-Maya cultures to the south and east. We should not forget that most of the early hieroglyphic writing found in the Maya area is from the Pacific foothills, at sites such as Abaj Takalik and El Baúl; the Copanecs need not necessarily have looked to the Petén to learn how to inscribe their monuments. Long Count dates and royal portraits had been carved in the highlands and Pacific Coast for three centuries before they were widely adopted in the southern lowlands. It would therefore be prudent to see the early Copán kingdom and its public displays as a fusion of a long-standing highland tradition (established at Copán) and sporadic lowland inputs.

With the onset of the Acbi phase, Copán had the cultural characteristics used to define 'Classic' Maya civilization: monumental architecture, stelae with inscribed hieroglyphic texts containing dates in the Long Count system, elaborate polychrome pottery, and a society governed by divine or semi-divine rulers. By the end of the Middle Classic period the population is estimated to have numbered between 8000 and 12,000, and Copán was emerging as one of the premier Maya regal-ritual cities. At the beginning of this period, however, it was at most half that size. For this reason, Sanders and many others object to calling the earliest Copán rulers 'kings'. They governed a nucleated, growing population, just beginning to organize itself along hierarchical lines. From this perspective, it would be more accurate to consider Copán during the first half of its recorded history (*c.* AD 435–635) a chiefdom rather than a state. It is to this important time in Copán's history that we now turn.

CHAPTER FIVE

THE PATH TO STATEHOOD

Political evolution and the case of the Maya

Anthropologists pursue the study of human cultures on two levels: the documentation and analysis of a particular society for its own sake; and the comparative or cross-cultural study of that society with others in the search for 'universals' of human behavior. For the purposes of cross-cultural analysis, certain levels or stages of organization of human society have been defined as a heuristic device to facilitate comparisons between groups of people who attained similar degrees of economic and socio-political complexity. The levels or stages thus defined have varied considerably over time, from the three defined by the 19th-century English sociologist Herbert Spencer (savagery, barbarism, and civilization), to the seven outlined by Lewis Henry Morgan (founder of American anthropology), and to others proposed more recently by Morton Fried and by Elman Service. Some contemporary archaeologists find the formulation of Service – which differentiates bands, tribes, chiefdoms, and states – one of the easiest to work with in the study of past societies as reconstructed from their material remains. There has been a great deal of debate as to what, precisely, serves to define these levels, but the stages themselves are useful for defining the parameters to be measured in the comparative analysis of socio-political evolution.

For our purposes here, let us define a 'chiefdom' as a society which has at least two socio-economic levels, ruled by a 'chief' who has responsibility for adjudicating disputes and for redistributing the resources of his people so that the community as a whole can prosper, oftentimes resulting in the institutionalization of succession from father to son. We will consider 'state' level societies as those which have populations in excess of 10,000 people; a central place for the operation of an institutionalized governing apparatus run by a professional ruling class; a hierarchy of four settlement (and administrative) levels with a concomitant hierarchy for the distribution of goods, services, and information; a monopoly on the use of force, if not the maintenance of a standing army; and a political organization including institutionalized offices wholly or partially divorced from kinship ties.[1]

In the case of Copán we have the advantage of both written records and considerable archaeological data on the size and makeup of the supporting population with which to chart the processes resulting in the development of a larger, more hierarchically-ordered kingdom. The first half of the recorded history of the city, in the opinion of the author, saw the development of the important institutions and societal changes that fostered population growth and nucleation, and the centralization of power, to the point that Copán became a state.

The rise of the Copán chiefdom

In the last chapter the evidence indicated that the transition from the Bijac to the Acbi ceramic phase (*c.* AD 400) included a number of important changes in Copán society, changes that can be used to justify the label of 'chiefdom' for 5th-century Copán. Evidence from both Group 9N-8 and the Principal Group showed that there were two different socio-economic levels in Copán society. The élite lived in plaster-coated, dressed masonry structures in close proximity to the decorated public buildings in the Principal Group, and had access to fine imported goods in ceramics and shell. The non-élite of Group 9N-8 and of other sites in the valley resided at some distance from the Principal Group, lived in cobblestone constructions, and were buried with relatively modest ceramic offerings. Likewise, there is clear evidence for institutionalized rulership (or chiefdom organization) in the form of the early hieroglyphic monuments; and in the public architecture of the earliest ballcourt (dated the latter half of the 4th century AD) and the adjacent buildings buried beneath Structure 10L-26 and the East Court of the Acropolis. Although the amount of large-scale excavation conducted to date does not allow us to demonstrate the patterns or timing of redistribution of resources carried out by the ruler, the elaboration of the architecture and the presence of written texts documenting his achievements leave little doubt that such redistribution was one of the many duties (and perquisites) assumed by the early Acbi phase rulers. The epigraphic evidence that the third and fourth Copán rulers controlled Quiriguá (and possibly the jade source in the Lower Motagua Valley, see below) indicates that their control of resources and redistributive power extended far beyond the limits of the Copán Valley.

The question of whether there was institutionalized primogeniture in the earliest Maya kingdoms, of whether the office of ruler or 'chief' ('halach uinic', or 'true man', to the 16th-century Yucatec Maya) was automatically passed from father to eldest son, is difficult to resolve. In the inscriptions of the Late Classic period, rulers at several different sites identified themselves clearly as the sons of the preceding rulers in identifiable parentage statements. Many other rulers, however – including some of those at Copán – did not detail their genealogy in hieroglyphic texts.

In the case of Copán, we are at a double disadvantage when attempting to resolve this question for the earliest period of recorded history: most of the earliest inscribed stone monuments were broken and buried by the fill of later constructions, making the texts not only hard to find, but fragmented and incomplete in most cases. At present, the contemporary Middle Classic inscriptions we have do not yet represent all twelve of the rulers which later monuments inform us reigned during the years from AD 426 to 695.

Recent tunnel excavations into the pyramidal platform of Structure 10L-26 uncovered a monument that helps to resolve the question of the nature of royal genealogy at Copán. Stela 63, and several later Copán monuments, provide abundant evidence that all the Middle and Late Classic Copán rulers claim to be from the same dynasty as the important 5th-century ruler K'inich Ahau Yax K'uk Mo'. The later hieroglyphic texts of the 7th and 8th centuries refer to events and persons in the past, and have in all known cases been corroborated by the records carved on the earlier monuments. We have no evidence in Copán, as yet, of extensive 'rewriting of history' on the part of later rulers, such as was often practiced among the competing dynasties of ancient Egypt, or by the Mexica Aztec under their Emperor Itzcoatl. What we know about the dynastic history of the site at this point is summarized in the following table:

The Founder: K'inich Yax K'uk Mo' (Mah K'ina Yax K'uk Mo')
Accession and death dates are unknown

Important dates:	8.19.10.0.0	9 Ahau	3 Muan	1 Feb	426
	8.19.10.10.17	5 Caban	15 Yaxkin	6 Sep	426
	8.19.10.11.0	8 Ahau	18 Yaxkin	9 Sep	426
	8.19.11.0.13	5 Ben	11 Muan	9 Feb	427
	9.0.0.0.0	8 Ahau	13 Ceh	11 Dec	435

Altar Q, West 2

Second in the succession
No contemporary monuments, save possibly Stela 24, according to Schele and Grube
Altar Q, West 1

Third in the succession: Mat Head
Accession and death dates are unknown
Monuments: Stela 63; cited on Monument 26, Quiriguá
Approximate date of reign: 9.0.10.0.0–9.2.10.0.0 (445–485)
Altar Q, North 4

Fourth in the succession: Cu Ix
Accession and death dates are unknown
Monuments: Step in Papagayo Structure; Monument 26, Quiriguá
Approximate date of reign: 9.2.10.0.0–9.3.0.0.0 (485–495)
Altar Q, North 3

Fifth and Sixth in the succession
No contemporary monuments known
Approximate date of reigns: 9.3.0.0.0–9.3.5.0.0 (495–500)
Altar Q, North 1 and 2

Seventh in the succession: Waterlily Jaguar

Accession:	9.?.?.?.?	13 Xul			
Important dates:	9.3.10.0.0	1 Ahau	8 Mac	9 Dec	504
	9.4.10.0.0	12 Ahau	8 Mol	26 Aug	504
	9.5.0.0.0	11 Ahau	18 Zec	5 Jul	534
	9.5.10.0.0	10 Ahau	8 Zip	13 May	544

Monuments: Stela 15; Stela E; cited on Caracol Stela 16
Altar Q, East 4; Hieroglyphic Stairway Steps 9, 55

Eighth in the succession

No contemporary monuments
Altar Q, East 3

Ninth in the succession

Accession: 9.5.17.13.7   2 Manik   0 Muan   30 Dec   551?
Altar Q, East 2; Hieroglyphic Stairway Step 18

Tenth in the succession: Moon Jaguar

Accession: 9.5.19.3.0   8 Ahau   3 Mac   26 May   553
Death: 9.7.4.17.4   10 Kan   2 Ceh   26 Oct   578
Monuments: Stela 9 (9.6.10.0.0, 29 Jan, 564); Ante Structure?
Altar Q, East 1; Hieroglyphic Stairway, Step 9

Eleventh in the succession: Butz' Chan

Birth: 9.6.9.4.6   7 Cimi   19 Uo   30 Apr   563
Accession: 9.7.5.0.8   8 Lamat   6 Mac   19 Nov   578
Death: 9.9.14.16.9   3 Muluc   2 Kayab   23 Jan   628
Monuments: Stela 7; Stela P; Altar Y; Rosalila Structure?
Altar Q, South 4; Hieroglyphic Stairway Step 8

Twelfth in the succession: Smoke Imix God K ('Smoke Jaguar')

Accession: 9.9.14.17.5   6 Chicchan 18 Kayab   8 Feb   628
Death: 9.13.3.5.7   12 Manik   0 Yaxkin   18 Jun   695
Monuments: Stelae 1; 2; 3; 5; 6; 10; 12; 13; 19; Altars H'; I'; K; Esmeralda Structure?; cited on Quiriguá Altar L
Altar Q, South 3; Hieroglyphic Stairway Steps 6–7

Thirteenth in the succession: 18 Rabbit ('XVIII-Jog')

Accession: 9.13.3.6.8   7 Lamat   1 Mol   9 Jul   695
Death: 9.15.6.14.6   6 Cimi   4 Zec   3 May   738
Monuments: Stelae A; B; C; D; F; H; J; 4; Altar S; Structures 10L-2; 10L-4; 10L-9 and 10 (Ballcourt A-III); 10L-22; 10L-26 3rd?
Altar Q, South 2; Hieroglyphic Stairway Steps 30, 38, 58, 61

Fourteenth in the succession: Smoke Monkey

Accession: 9.15.6.16.5   6 Chicchan 3 Yaxkin   11 Jun   738
Death: 9.15.17.12.16   10 Cib   4 Uayeb   4 Feb   749
Monument: Structure 10L-22A (the *Popol Na*)
Altar Q, South 1; Hieroglyphic Stairway Steps 39, 40, 41, 43, 54

Fifteenth in the succession: Smoke Shell ('Smoke Squirrel')

Accession: 9.15.17.13.10   11 Oc   13 Pop   18 Feb   749
Monuments: Stela M; Stela N; Hieroglyphic Stairway (and Temple) of Structure 10L-26
Altar Q, West 4; Hieroglyphic Stairway Steps 37, 39, 40

Sixteenth in the succession: Yax Pac ('Yax "Sun-at-Horizon"'; 'New Dawn'; 'First Dawn'; 'Madrugada'; etc.)

Accession: 9.16.12.5.17   6 Caban   10 Mol   2 Jul   763
Death: c.9.19.10.0.0   8 Ahau   8 Xul   6 May   820

Monuments: Stela 8; Stela 11 (posthumous), Altars G1; G2; G3; D'; O; Q; R; T; U; V; Z;
inscribed stone from Str. 10L-22A; Structures 10L-11; 10L-16; 10L-18; 10L-21A; cited on
inscriptions from numerous stone incense burner lids and other texts from the valley,
including those from Structures 10L-32; 9N-82, CV 43A; and Altar W'
Altar Q, West 3

Final pretender to the throne: U Cit Tok'
Supposed
accession: 9.19.11.14.5   3 Chicchan 3 Uo   10 Feb   822
Monument: Altar L (U Cit Tok' shown on south side, left figure)

Yax K'uk Mo', the founder of the Copán dynasty

The earliest dated inscribed monument at Copán, Stela 63, was recently
discovered by my students Joel Palka and Richard Williamson in the buried
structure given the field name 'Papagayo'. The central inscription of Stela 63
carries the Maya Long Count date 9.0.0.0.0 8 Ahau 14 [sic] Ceh, corresponding
to 11 December AD 435. Found in three pieces, the stela had been broken and
buried inside the building where it had originally been erected. The butt of the
stela was still *in situ*, showing that the monument had been placed against the
back wall of the inner chamber of the building, in a similar way to the nearly
contemporaneous Stela 1 at Lamanai.[2] Stratigraphic evidence for continuous
use of this building through several modifications of the ballcourt and adjacent
floors and buildings, and the types of ceramics found in the fill – dating the time
of destruction and burial of the structure and its stela – indicate that the ritual
'killing' of both building and stela took place nearly two centuries after the
commemorative date of Stela 63.

An error in the lunar age inscribed in the Initial Series led the project
epigraphers to suggest that the citation of the 9.0.0.0.0 date was retrospective,
and that the scribes had made an error in their computation of the lunar age.
This hypothesis is supported by the fact that the son of the protagonist of the
9.0.0.0.0 event was apparently the one who dedicated this stela. On the north
side of the stela the son cites his own name in conjunction with what is
probably the dedication verb, followed by the 'child of father' glyph, and the
name K'inich Yax K'uk Mo', which is the name cited in association with the
9.0.0.0.0 date of the Initial Series date.

This monument was carved as a retrospective commemoration of the
completion of one of the most important calendrical cycles for the Maya, the
baktun, or period of 400 approximate (360-day) years. In this case the stela
marks the completion of the 9th *baktun* since the beginning of the present era,
calculated to have begun in the year 3114 BC. This 'Period Ending' was a
particularly important one, akin to what the year AD 2000 will be for Western
civilization: a time-marker, a point at which to pause and reflect on one's
achievements as well as one's challenges for the future. This was a period of

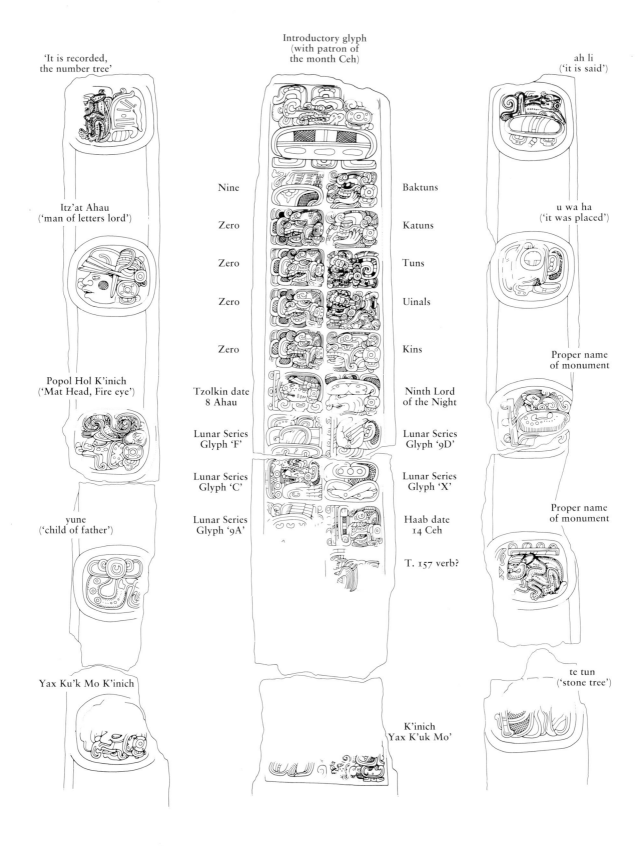

'It is recorded, the number tree'

Introductory glyph
(with patron of
the month Ceh)

ah li
('it is said')

Itz'at Ahau
('man of letters lord')

Nine — Baktuns

u wa ha
('it was placed')

Zero — Katuns

Popol Hol K'inich
('Mat Head, Fire eye')

Zero — Tuns

Zero — Uinals

Proper name
of monument

Zero — Kins

Tzolkin date
8 Ahau — Ninth Lord
of the Night

yune
('child of father')

Lunar Series
Glyph 'F' — Lunar Series
Glyph '9D'

Lunar Series
Glyph 'C' — Lunar Series
Glyph 'X'

Proper name
of monument

Lunar Series
Glyph '9A' — Haab date
14 Ceh

T. 157 verb?

Yax Ku'k Mo K'inich

te tun
('stone tree')

K'inich
Yax K'uk Mo'

Stela 63

37 (Opposite) Stela 63.

38 Interior of Papagayo Structure, buried inside the pyramidal base of Structure 10L-26. The upper portion of Stela 63 is visible on the right, wedged between the front and back walls of the building. The stela originally stood behind the hieroglyphic step at the back of the room.

39 (Below) The upper portion of Stela 63, as it was found in Papagayo Structure. The inscription carries the Long Count date 9.0.0.0.0 8 Ahau 14 Ceh (AD 435).

great intellectual ferment in the Maya lowlands, corresponding to the beginning of the spread of inscribed stone monuments with Long Count dates to areas outside the north-central Petén, core area for the Classic Maya tradition.

In Copán, apparently the event commemorated on Stela 63 was of such importance that future generations of rulers continued to cite it in the most prominent of their public monuments. References to the date 9.0.0.0.0, or to the event ('display of the Manikin Scepter') and its protagonist (Yax K'uk Mo') appear on Stela 15, commemorated by the 7th ruler Waterlily Jaguar, and on Stela J, the accession monument of the 13th ruler 18 Rabbit. The event and protagonist are also cited on the king's list and legitimation monument of the 16th ruler, Yax Pac, on the text on the top of Altar Q. These later records are very helpful, because the verb associated with the 9.0.0.0.0 date on the basal part of Stela 63 was obliterated when the monument was deliberately broken.

Still, Yax K'uk Mo's name appears on the butt of the stela and, as it was found *in situ*, there is no question but that he is the protagonist of the 9.0.0.0.0 date. The later citations of this date, event, and ruler are also important in that they show that the subsequent rulers took this to be the base-line of their dynastic history. In the project epigraphers' view, this event was the one which later rulers used to justify the view that Yax K'uk Mo' was the founder of their dynasty.[3] Each subsequent ruler cites himself as the 'successor of Yax K'uk Mo', founder of Copán', and on Altar Q Yax Pac portrays the founder and each of the 15 rulers in the line of succession.

The stratigraphic evidence shows clearly that the commemoration of Stela 63 corresponds with the construction of Papagayo Structure itself. The upper part of the building on the front and sides was destroyed when it was buried, at least a century later, but the back side still retains part of the upper register of the original façade. On it was an extraordinary image modeled in stucco and extending across the entire rear of the building. It is an enormous crocodile, complete with reptilian belly scales, shown in profile with head to the south and tail to the north. The saurian is modeled in high relief and internal stone supports were placed inside the stucco so that the head and limbs actually protruded from the plane of the façade by about 40 cm. The crocodile is shown floating above signs for water and stone, indicating that the Middle Classic Copanecs shared the larger Mesoamerican view that the surface of the earth was the back of a giant crocodile, floating in an immense pond. When the ruler performed ceremonies in the context of this imagery, he was being placed in a scale model of the Maya world, upon which he was the center of attention, both mortal and supernatural. The construction of this icon indicates the increasing complexity of functions carried out by the chiefdom and the pursuit of other types of religious ritual, the ultimate purpose of which was to consolidate the prestige and power of the rulers who sponsored and participated in those rituals.

Some time after the first construction phase of Ballcourt A and Papagayo Structure, a large pyramidal building was constructed to the south of it, the remains of which are still preserved underneath the later versions of Temple 11. From the 5th century AD onward, then, an open courtyard area was bounded by the ballcourt on the north, an early version of Structure 10L-26 on the east, and an early version of Structure 10L-11 on the south. This assemblage remained the same throughout the history of the Principal Group; and although there were changes in size, orientation, and decoration, the present evidence indicates that the functions of these three structures were also consistent. The two structures forming the ballcourt defined the playing ground for the rubber ballgame; Structure 10L-26 always served as a dynastic temple, related to ancestor worship and its accompanying rituals; and Structure 11 was a lineage or rulership house, according to the inscriptions found on two different stages of the building.[4]

In Maya society most sacred propositions remained constant through time.

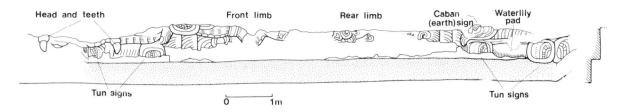

40 The back (east) side of Papagayo Structure, showing the crocodile modeled in stucco, and the earth and waterlily signs.

The playing of a rubber ball game in Mesoamerica began in the Early Preclassic, and it is therefore fitting that a formal court in which to play ball was amongst the first of the temples constructed at Copán. Accounts of the ballgame by 16th-century Spanish observers, and analysis of the imagery found carved in stone on the ballcourts or painted on polychrome pots of the Classic period, indicate that the ritual purpose of the Maya ballgame was to ensure the perpetuation of natural cycles and fertility: specifically the movements of the sun, moon, heavenly bodies, and the agricultural cycle. By sponsoring and perhaps participating in ritual 'combat' in the ballcourt, the ruler was seen to be helping to keep the world on track. Ballcourts have also been found at Late Preclassic Maya sites such as Cerros, Belize, and seem to have formed an important component of the complex of public buildings which served as the focus of Maya kingdoms.

The Mesoamerican ballgame had a complex set of rules according to 16th-century chroniclers. The basic idea was to keep the ball in play by bouncing it off the sloped surfaces or 'benches' that formed the two sides of the court, using one's hips and knees. Special protective gear was worn by the players (illus. 69), since the ball was made of solid rubber, and thus very hard. The ball was not allowed to touch the central, depressed floor or 'playing alley', because it was believed that this would rouse and anger the Lords of the Underworld. Players scored points by knocking the ball into the open area or 'end zone' of their opponents' end of the court. (During the Postclassic period a new twist was added: a ring was placed above the center of each bench, and if a player somehow managed to pass the ball through the ring the game was won.) In Copán, all versions of Ballcourt A had three sculpted macaw-head stone 'markers' inset into the top of each inclined bench parallel to the playing alley, one placed at each end, and one in the middle. Stone markers were also set into the middle and each end of the central axis of the playing alley, presumably used for line markers or perhaps for scoring points, though exactly how this was done is not presently known.

Analysis of 16th-century descriptions of the game, and comparison with versions that have survived to this day in parts of rural Mexico, would suggest that the rules were designed so that most games would end in a tie. When

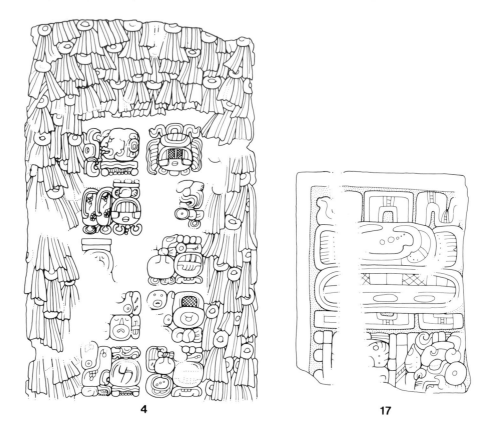

4   17

41 References to the 8.6.0.0.0 10 Ahau 13 Ch'en (AD 159) Period Ending in Copán, on Stelae I, 4, and 17. Stela I also refers to the emblem-glyph of Copán in association with a date some 200 days later, leading Linda Schele to believe that this date was associated with the founding of the kingdom.

I

someone actually won a game, it was therefore a source of great excitement and wonder. An episode in the Sacred Book of the Quiché Maya, the *Popol Vuh*, tells of a ballgame between the Hero Twins and the Lords of the Underworld, in which the stunning victory of the Twins was seen as a staggering defeat over the masters of hell. It is believed that on important ceremonial occasions, Maya rulers took on the role of the Hero Twins, and their opponents took on the role (and perhaps even the costume) of the Lords of the Underworld (illus. 69). If the ruler won the game, he symbolically defeated the forces of death, darkness, disease, and famine, giving his people cause to rejoice.

One intriguing aspect of the historical record is that later monuments show that Yax K'uk Mo' was not the first ruler of Copán, although he was the founder of the most famous dynasty. On Stela I, the 7th ruler states that Yax K'uk Mo' was himself the 'successor of Smoke Codex God K'. Stela 24 has a Long Count date of 9.2.10.0.0 (AD 485) on its front side, but cites another individual, called 'first to be seated', in the text on the back side, presumably associated with an earlier date. On the basis of Stela 24's Long Count date,

Morley concluded that the area presently occupied by the village of Copán Ruinas was the earliest center of habitation and monument commemoration in the valley. The new decipherment of the non-calendric glyphs on the back of Stela 24 seem to support this view. Another earlier ruler is indicated by the Period Ending date '1 Ahau 8 Ch'en' recorded on the Peccary Skull placed in Tomb 1 (see page 52): 8.17.0.0.0, or AD 377. The scene shows two seated personages facing a stela and altar, and one of the individuals is named by accompanying glyphs as 'Leaf Ahau'.

a

Early historical references are also found on the much later monuments of Stelae 4 and I, where there are references to the dates 8.6.0.0.0 and 8.6.0.10.8 respectively, falling in the years AD 159 and 160. Associated with the later date is an individual named 'Ma K'ina Ya Yo Ahau' (the latter part of the name resembling the 'Leaf Ahau' on the Peccary Skull text), followed by the Copán emblem-glyph. Given the Mesoamerican-wide practice of compiling and conserving historical codices documented in the Maya area as late as the 17th century by López de Cogolludo,[5] these references to earlier historical events should not be dismissed out of hand as 'legendary' or 'mythical'; it is probable that there is some basis in fact to them. And the nature of the archaeological evidence for the people residing around the Principal Group at that time implies that history was being made there. Yet another earlier date, 7.1.13.15.0 9 Ahau 13 Cumku (355 BC), is cited on Altar I; but whether such an early event was mythical, legendary, or real I would not hazard to surmise.

b

c

Early successors of the founder

Whatever the nature of the political organization of the rulers who preceded Yax K'uk Mo', it was from his reign forward that Copán prospered as a cohesive political unit. As noted, the son of Yax K'uk Mo' was responsible for the dedication of Stela 63. It has been suggested that Stela 63 contains a title for the 3rd ruler that reads *itz'at* ('learned man'; 'sage'; 'man of letters'), a title also claimed by the 4th ruler on the hieroglyphic step that he had placed in front of Stela 63. This indicates the importance of literacy and knowledge to these early Copán rulers.[6] Recently, Schele has reinterpreted the text on the second earliest stela at Quiriguá (Monument 26, *c*. AD 493). She notes that two individuals are cited on the early Quiriguá text as the '3rd ruler' and '4th ruler'. The name of the individual associated with the '3rd ruler' reference is the same as that cited on Copán Stela 63 as the son of Yax K'uk Mo'. The name of the individual cited as the '4th ruler' on Quiriguá Monument 26 is also found on an inscribed

d

e

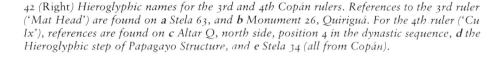

42 (Right) *Hieroglyphic names for the 3rd and 4th Copán rulers. References to the 3rd ruler ('Mat Head') are found on* **a** *Stela 63, and* **b** *Monument 26, Quiriguá. For the 4th ruler ('Cu Ix'), references are found on* **c** *Altar Q, north side, position 4 in the dynastic sequence,* **d** *the Hieroglyphic step of Papagayo Structure, and* **e** *Stela 34 (all from Copán).*

hieroglyphic step, placed directly in front of Copán Stela 63, in the inner chamber of Papagayo Structure. No native Quiriguá ruler is cited on the Monument 26 text, nor is there any mention of the Quiriguá emblem-glyph. The implication is clear: Copán controlled Quiriguá, from at least the time of the 3rd and 4th Copán rulers. The lucrative Motagua jade route was probably the reason for Copán's interest in this area.

The hieroglyphic step bearing the name of the 4th Copán ruler ('Cu Ix') was placed inside Papagayo Structure at the same time that a second floor was laid down inside the building. The step and its floor covered the original floor, which was contemporaneous with the commemoration of Stela 63 and the actual construction of Papagayo Structure itself. Cu Ix's name appears on the riser of the hieroglyphic step, third glyph from the right; most of the more extensive inscription on the top (including the commemoration date) was destroyed when the monument was ritually 'killed' toward the beginning of the 7th century AD. The name inscribed on the step corresponds to the one under the fourth personage in the succession on Altar Q, and on a contemporary Middle Classic monument, Stela 46. The hieroglyphic step inside Papagayo Structure was battered and burned in the ceremony when Stela 63 and the building were buried, along with six early ballcourt markers in the shape of macaw heads, which were placed in the fill inside the structure.

There are other carved stone monuments which may be contemporary with Papagayo Structure, Ballcourt A-I, and Structure 10L-sub-2. Stela 35, discovered in the fill of Structure 10L-4 of the Great Plaza, was dated by Claude Baudez, on the basis of its style, c. AD 400.[7] This would place its carving slightly before that of Stela 63. This fragment of Stela 35 has no inscription, but the figure bears the serpent-bodied 'ceremonial bar', the conventional badge of Maya rulers during the Classic period; and Schele believes that Stela 35 may be a portrait of Yax K'uk Mo'.[8] The next stela in stylistic sequence, Stela 60, has parts of hieroglyphic texts on its sides, and part of a human portrait on the front. The ceremonial bar is again present, though in more rigid, less naturalistic form than that seen on Stela 35.

Perspectives from the valley

In addition to the evidence for an increasingly complex society from the inscriptions and architectural monuments of the Principal Group, there exists abundant archaeological evidence for population growth and diversification in the Copán Valley during the Middle Classic period. This comes from the valley-wide test-pit excavations, from more extensive excavations at Group 9N-8, from excavations in various parts of the Principal Group, and from the investigation of a site known locally as 'el Cerro de las Mesas', located 1 km north of the modern village.[9] (The site of Cerro de las Mesas lies on the razed top of a heavily terraced mountain, which was clearly designed to be defensible. It is not known whether this was to defend its occupants from

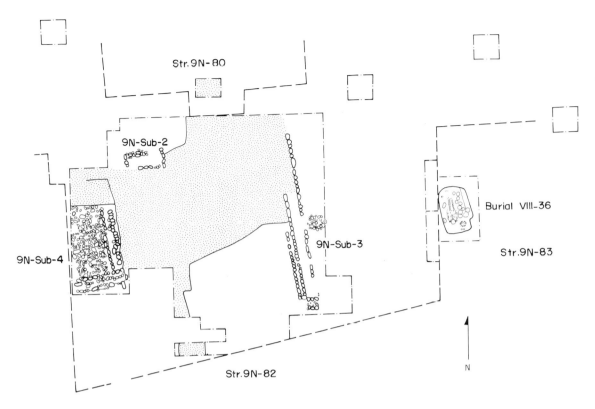

Str. 9N-80

9N-Sub-2

9N-Sub-4

9N-Sub-3

Burial VIII-36

Str. 9N-83

Str. 9N-82

N

43 *Plan of Group 9N-8, Patio A, during the Middle Classic period (Acbi ceramic phase).*

enemies from within or without the valley, but it does indicate a certain preoccupation with defense during the Middle Classic period.)

Middle Classic remains are constantly being unearthed by the modern villagers when digging on their private house lots. In fact, the extent of Middle Classic remains in the modern village and at Cerro de las Mesas is of such a magnitude that the two locations may represent the remains of two 'great families' (socio-economically powerful extended families and their allied kin and retainers) of the 5th and 6th centuries AD.[10] We have already noted that the Principal Group of ruins was the seat of divine authority for the ruler. But is it possible that the ruler was selected from among several competing royal or noble lineages with rival claims to the throne?

The excavations at Group 9N-8 also revealed some interesting Middle Classic remains. Plaza floor III in Patio A was a plaster floor shared by three buildings, grouped around an open plaza or patio. Remembering that the Early Classic (Bijac phase) constructions here were purely of cobble and earth, the addition of plaster seems to indicate a step up the social scale for the occupants in the Middle Classic. A midden (refuse heap) containing domestic pottery,

44 *View of Burial VIII-36, showing overlying strata and its context beneath the final-phase Structure 9N-83 of Patio A, Group 9N-8.*

45 (Opposite, above) *Detail of Burial VIII-36. The weight of the overlying strata had crushed the ceramic vessels long before the burial was uncovered in 1981.*

46 (Opposite, below) *Plan of Burial VIII-36, showing the placement of offerings on the plaster floor. The sting-ray spines, tortoise shells, and special stones are all indicative of religious rites.*

Burial VIII-36

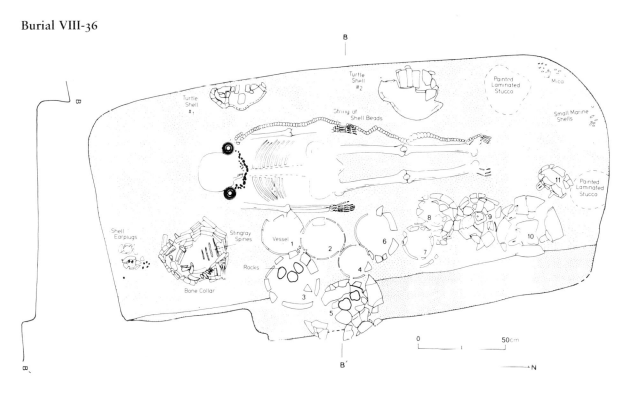

burned earth, and carbon was found on the western edge of the plaza floor, indicating that food was prepared at the site, possibly in the small (1.5 × 2.2 m) structure located at the northwest corner of the plaza. The Middle Classic building on the east side of the plaza measured 17 m north–south by 6 m east–west, and was entered by a step on its west, patio-facing side. This was probably the most important building on the site at this time. And buried just to the east and beneath it was its most important occupant.

Designated Burial VIII-36, this Middle Classic resident of Group 9N-8 was clearly a distinguished and revered individual in 5th-century Copán society. Estimated to have been about 45 years old at the time of his death, this man measured 1.7 m in height, above the average height of modern-day Maya Indians and suggestive of superior nutrition. He was buried with considerable care and circumstance, a reflection not just of his prestige, but also of his livelihood: for it would appear this man was a shaman. Buried with him were all the utensils associated with an individual who practiced religious rituals: sting-ray spines used in auto-sacrificial rites; the bones of his animal spirit companions (*naguales*) – the deer and the cayman – through whom he entered the spirit world; a codex or bark-paper book, presumably alive with the auguries and sacred lore of his day, but now hopelessly deteriorated; and five peculiar quartz stones, with ferromagnesium inclusions, probably used in divination rituals. (Writing in the 16th century, Fray (later Bishop) Diego de Landa wrote that 'if he was a sorcerer, they buried with him some of his stones for witchcraft and instruments of his profession'.)[11] In the case of this burial, the five stones were found in two adjacent Usulutan Ware mammiform tetrapod bowls – two in one bowl and three in the other. These bowls have simple curvilinear designs in their interiors which were produced by some sort of 'negative' or 'resist' decorative technique, and have four supports on their underside in the shape of female breasts. The handle of one of these bowls was adorned with a wizened human face, and one wonders if this is a portrait of the shaman himself.

(The local people in the village of Copán became convinced that we had, indeed, discovered the remains of a shaman when I suffered a serious injury a week after discovering the burial, and after a complicated operation returned to Copán in a hip-to-toe cast. To this day the burial is known locally as 'el Brujo' (the warlock), and when a tragedy befalls a member of the community it is often blamed on him. Even in death he is a social force to be contended with, for when the rumor circulated that he was to be removed from Copán for temporary display in the capital city while the local museum was under renovation, there was nearly a riot on the village square. The burial literally had to be smuggled out of the village under cover of darkness! Now he resides (peacefully, we hope) with all his offerings in the Copán Museum.)

The burial is of interest not just in itself, but also for what it tells us about the evolution of society in the Copán Valley. The shaman was obviously of much higher status than his predecessors of the Bijac phase. In the burial, the number and quality of imported, high-quality craft goods (which included the lidded, basal flange, polychrome bowls – probably imported from the highlands of Guatemala – 110 spondylus shell beads, a cayman tooth and deer mandible necklace, and a jade necklace) demonstrate that he had moved to a higher socio-economic level. But was his status acquired – achieved through his own efforts and skills in the art of curing and divination – or ascribed – the result of his having been born the son of a wealthy individual? This question is one which archaeologists often confront, because ascribed status implies formal ranking of the members of a society, whereas acquired status does not. Although his height argues for at least some element of ascribed status, the lack of any impressive grave goods with the earlier burials found at the site justifies the view that at least part of this individual's status was acquired. And there were extensive hypoplasias (evidence of arrested dental development) on his teeth enamel suggesting to physical anthropologist Rebecca Storey that he suffered a difficult childhood. This evidence for acquired status in early Copán supports the view expressed long ago by William Rathje that between AD 250 and 600 Maya society was more fluid, with greater possibilities for social mobility than in the Late Classic, when social rankings became fixed (presumably along blood-lines).[12]

Middle Classic burials from the Principal Group

The excavations conducted at the Principal Group have also uncovered a number of Middle Classic period human burials, many of them quite impressive in terms of grave goods – none more so than Burial V-6, discovered by Juan Antonio Valdez and Charles Cheek in their investigations of the area just north of Structure 10L-26. This individual, also an adult male, was buried in a seated position in a stone cist several meters below the level of the Late Classic plaza floor, near the central axis of Structure 10L-26. Although there are no inscriptions to identify him by name, the quantity and quality of the grave goods, along with the placement of the grave near one of the most sacred buildings in the Principal Group, indicates that he was probably either a member of the royal family, or of the ruler's court. Among the offerings were: a bowl of so-called Thin Orange ware imported from Central Mexico (possibly from Teotihuacan, the great trading metropolis north of Mexico City, perhaps via Kaminaljuyu, considered by many to have been a Teotihuacano outpost); an exquisitely carved bowl, with iconic designs in Kaminaljuyu style; numerous other ceramic vessels; hundreds of pieces of shell; a slate-back iron pyrite mirror; finely polished pieces of jade; and other goods.

Another important individual was buried directly beneath the large plaster sculpture on the east side of a large platform located due east of Papagayo Structure, and pre-dating the latter by one construction phase. This building consisted of a large platform, crowned by a superstructure that was obliterated by later construction. At least the eastern side of the platform was adorned

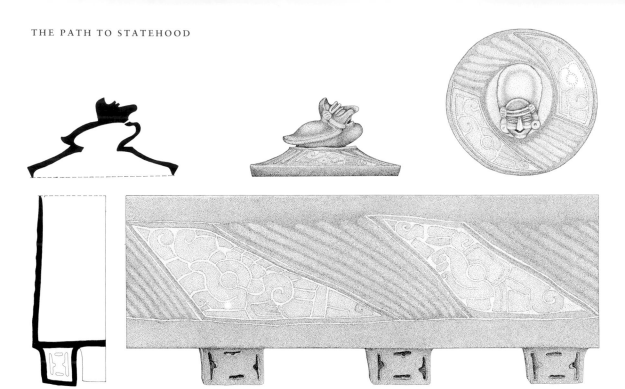

47 *Ceramic vessel from Burial XXXVII-1, showing quetzal and macaw birds incised on the vessel body and lid. Height 23 cm.*

with plaster sculpture masks of the deity referred to as 'G1', upon whose head is perched a bird with outstretched wings. Burial XXXVII-1 consisted of an aged woman placed on her back, head to the south, in a stone cist built directly below and in front of the plaster mask. She was given the benefit of 3 ceramic vessels, 2 large pieces of jade (one in the mouth, the pan-Mesoamerican custom for ensuring that the deceased's soul would go to heaven), 4 pieces of shell, 2 unused obsidian bladelets, and 2 bone sewing needles. The incised decoration on the body and lid of one of the ceramic vessels may identify this woman by name, or at least by ancestry. Both the cylindrical tripod vessel and its lid carry two birds, anatomically identifiable as the quetzal (*k'uk*, in Maya) and the scarlet macaw (*mo'*). Since the inscribed pot reads, literally, K'uk Mo', could it be that the woman represented in Burial XXXVII-1 was related to the distinguished Yax K'uk Mo' himself? In any case, the placement of the burial in front of such a powerful icon implies the occupant's special place in ancient Copán society.

Burial XXXVII-2 was placed directly east of Burial XXXVII-1: an adult male in a stone-lined cist with capstones. The skeleton of this individual constitutes the most robust physical specimen of over 500 thus far recovered at Copán. Buried with him was a single, rather austere vessel, again dating to the early part of the Middle Classic period. More significant than the vessel was the jade bead found in his mouth. In this case, the bead was carved in the form of what epigraphers refer to as the *ti* vulture, which is read as *ahau* (lord). This robust male, then, was considered a lord at Middle Classic Copán.

Some time after the placement of Burials XXXVII-1 and XXXVII-2, the platform east of Papagayo Structure, and the burial cists, were covered over in the construction of Mascarón Structure. This building, also, had large plaster masks, at least on the front (west) side, and a central staircase providing access to a temple on top. Stromsvik had originally uncovered the northern of these two masks, in his 1939 tunneling operations under the Hieroglyphic Stairway.[13] To the west of the central steps was Papagayo Structure, which was built at the same time, during the reign of the third ruler.

In the Acropolis, new investigations of the Acbi phase constructions in the Archaeological Cut and adjacent East Court structures are being carried out by Robert Sharer and David Sedat of the University of Pennsylvania. Their excavations are revealing major construction complexes dating from the beginning of the Middle Classic to the end of the recorded history of the site. The study of the eastern face of the Acropolis – carved out by the Copán River – is now being extended underneath the final phase architecture of the East Court, and has revealed five major construction phases. Each phase included numerous buildings on the east, west, and north sides, and the likelihood that there was a contemporary version of Structure 16, as well. Several buildings have yielded important decorative elements, such as the plaster masks on the apron-molding façades of 'Ante Structure' and the painted glyphic text on 'Parrot Structure', which Sharer and his colleagues believe may have been used by Yax K'uk Mo' himself. To the south of these lay the massive 'Amarillo' Structure, comprising one of the largest monuments ever erected at Copán – clear evidence of the power of the early Copán rulers. Doubtless the continuing

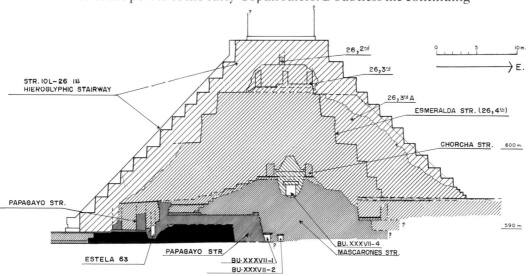

48 Cross-section of Structure 10L-26 as revealed by the tunnels, showing buildings referred to in the text.

work here will resolve whether the buildings in the East Court were as traditional in layout and focus as those of the group comprising Ballcourt A, Structure 10L-26, and Structure 10L-11. Sharer and Sedat's work on the early Acropolis is sure to provide critical information on the history and nature of the functions and significance of these structures, to complement the sequence from the valley and other parts of the Principal Group.

Dynastic history in the 5th and 6th centuries

After the reign of the 4th ruler, Cu Ix, there are presently no known contemporary monuments for the 5th and 6th rulers, so there are no texts that provide us with historical data for these individuals. For the 7th ruler, Waterlily Jaguar, we have Stela 15 from Group 9, and Stela E from the Principal Group. The 7th ruler is the first for which we presently have monuments from both areas. Project epigrapher Nikolae Grube discovered that he is also the first Copán ruler to be cited on a monument outside of the southeast Maya zone, being mentioned on Stela 16 of the site of Caracol, Belize. In the view of Grube, this mention demonstrates that Copán was a politically dominant center in the Middle Classic and that it was somehow prestigious for the Caracol lord to mention his interactions with Waterlily-Jaguar of Copán. Stela E carries his portrait, which was allowed by later rulers to reside on the western edge of the steps on the west side of the Great Plaza. Waterlily Jaguar's known post-accession dates encompass the 40 years from AD 504 to 544, indicating a lengthy reign. Stela 15 cites the 9.0.0.0.0 event of Yax K'uk Mo'. For the 8th and 9th rulers we have no contemporary monuments, possibly owing to the fact that their combined reigns lasted only nine years.

The accession of the 10th ruler, 'Moon Jaguar', occurred on 9.5.19.3.0 (26 May AD 553). He is portrayed on Stela 9, which dates to AD 564, and on Stela 18 (AD 574). Both these monuments are from Group 9, indicating that this area was of great concern to him, but not necessarily meaning that other monuments dating to his reign do not lie buried under later constructions in the Principal Group. Stela 9 states that Moon Jaguar's father was Waterlily Jaguar, and thus raises the question of how the line of succession worked. Given the length of Waterlily Jaguar's reign, it seems plausible that the 8th and 9th rulers were also his sons, but that each died shortly after assuming the throne, and were succeeded by their younger brother, Moon Jaguar. Alternatively, the 8th and 9th rulers could have been the younger brothers of Waterlily Jaguar, each succumbing within a few years of the death of their long-lived older brother. This makes somewhat more sense biologically than the first hypothesis, when one considers that Moon Jaguar himself reigned for 25 years, before dying in AD 578. Agnatic succession is known to have occurred in Palenque, where there were four cases of the ruler being succeeded by his younger brother, rather than by his own son.

49 *Stela E, portrait of Waterlily Jaguar, above the steps on the west side of the Great Plaza. Note the elongation of the human figure; on the 8th-century stelae, the trunk is shortened, and the head is enlarged, as first noted by Spinden.*

Moon Jaguar was succeeded by another long-lived ruler, the 11th in the dynasty of Yax K'uk Mo', named Butz' Chan (Smoke Snake or Smoke Sky). Born in April AD 563, Butz' Chan acceded to power 15 years later, and reigned for 50 years before dying on 23 January AD 628. He is the second ruler for whom we have monuments in both the Principal Group (Stela P) and Group 9 (the area of the modern village – Stela 7). Stela P represents one of the finest Middle Classic monuments at Copán, and was incorporated in the final phase architecture in the West Court of the Acropolis. On it, Butz' Chan cites one of his titles with an *ah-po* (lord) superfix – a glyph also recorded on the Late Classic Stela 1 of Los Higos, a site located 70 km east of Copán. This may indicate some sort of dominion or personal involvement with Los Higos, if this title is taken as equivalent to an emblem-glyph (though it lacks the 'water group' prefix normally accompanying an emblem-glyph). David Stuart points

50, 51 (Left and opposite) Stela P, portrait of Butz' Chan. This stela was removed from its original location during the 8th century AD, and placed where it now stands, near the northeast corner of the West Court of the Acropolis.

out that it may simply mean that the same title (not an emblem-glyph) or 'attribute' was shared by Butz' Chan and the later individual portrayed on the Los Higos stela. Although we cannot state with certainty that this attribute in his name clause indicates that he subjugated or politically controlled the Los Higos area, at least we now know to look for archaeological and other epigraphic evidence that this might have been the case.

Evidence from the test-pits of PAC I indicates that the 7th century was one of marked population growth in the eastern half of the Copán pocket, and the expansion of the local supporting population could have served as the base from which Butz' Chan sought to expand his domain. In any case, all indications from the excavations of the earlier complex of Ballcourt A, Structure 10L-26, Structure 10L-11, and from the East Court of the Acropolis, are that building activities were renewed during his reign.

P

Another extraordinary Acropolis monument that may date to the reign of Butz' Chan is Rosalila Structure. Discovered by Copán Acropolis Archaeological Project Co-Director Ricardo Agurcia in the tunnels under Structure 10L-16, this magnificent edifice was very carefully preserved, and buried, by the ancient Maya – rather than smashed to pieces, as was the usual custom – prior to the construction of another building over it. As such, it is the only known example of a temple structure in Copán that has survived intact. The building measures 12 m east–west by 18 m north–south, and is two-storied, with a roof crest on top. This elegant structure is most remarkable in that it conserves virtually all of its original façade sculpture ornamentation, modeled in painted stucco. As such, it presents students of Classic Maya art with a wealth of iconographic detail and religious imagery for analysis and interpretation.[14]

Framing the doorway on Rosalila's west side are two large birds shown head-on, from whose open mouths emerge the head of the old god Itzamna (a primordial deity of the ancient Maya). Above the birds on the first-story entablature are inverted, stylized images of giant serpent heads. On the second story is a large deity head, flanked by *witz* (mountain) signs and the heads of two serpents, whose undulating bodies extend up into the roof crest. Also on the second story on the north side are images of the Perforator God, unquestionably related to sacrificial rituals. This last icon may be a key to understanding the imagery of the temple. Perhaps Rosalila Structure represents a sacred mountain (*witz*) associated with rites in honor of Itzamna, in whose honor blood was offered in sacrifice.

A truly extraordinary cache of sacred objects was found by Agurcia on the floor of the west room of Rosalila. Placed inside a roughly-constructed circular stone cist in the south end of the room, the offering consisted of 9 'eccentric' flints (so-called because of the diverse, eccentric shapes into which they were chipped), 3 lanceolate flint spear heads, 3 spiny oyster shells, 1 jade bead, a stingray spine, numerous baby shark vertebrae, and the remains of a brightly-dyed blue fabric that was used to wrap the entire offering. The eccentric flints were also individually wrapped in the blue cloth, portions of which adhered to the artifacts themselves. Six of the nine eccentrics are of exquisite workmanship and are very consistent in their decorative techniques. The author believes that they were fashioned by one individual, or at least by a single 'school' of flint-knappers, under the tutelage of a single master. The other three eccentric flints were the handiwork of a much less skilled artisan. The six more elaborate eccentric flints represent some of the finest chipped stone artifacts ever fashioned in antiquity.

The reign of Smoke Imix God K

The 12th ruler, Smoke Imix God K, acceded to power in AD 628, and reigned for 67 years. This long reign, although unusual, is documented on more standing monuments – both contemporary and retrospective – than we have

52 Elevation drawing of the west side of Rosalila Structure, showing the stucco façade sculpture uncovered in 1991.

for any other member of the Copán dynasty. He was in all likelihood the single most important individual ruler in the site's history, except possibly the founder Yax K'uk Mo'. In terms of his life-span, it is interesting to note that we have no standing monuments for the first 26 years of his reign, followed by a veritable explosion in the Period Ending 9.11.0.0.0 (AD 652). These data may indicate that as a young ruler, Smoke Imix God K took a certain amount of time to establish himself, but left a very strong imprint once he was firmly in control. Indeed, it was in the fifteenth year of his reign that he erected the famous set of six stelae in the Copán Valley.

Joseph Spinden was the first to point out the contemporaneity of dates on these six stelae – dedicated within 260 days of each other – and to interpret them as territorial markers placed on the limits of Copán's domain at that time.[15] Numerous subsequent writers have followed his way of thinking, but others have taken different points of view. Morley suggested that Stelae 10 and 12 might represent a sort of gigantic, valley-wide sun marker, set to 19 April – when the sun set behind Stela 10 on the western horizon, as viewed from Stela 12 at the eastern end of the valley – time to burn the fields in preparation for the planting season.[16] Proskouriakoff believed that the placement of the monuments at selected locations within the valley may have been an attempt to associate certain revered ancestors with particular sacred mountains.[17] As it happens, Yax K'uk Mo' is cited on Stelae 10 and 19. More recently, the author suggested that the placement of the stelae, at least in the eastern entrance to the

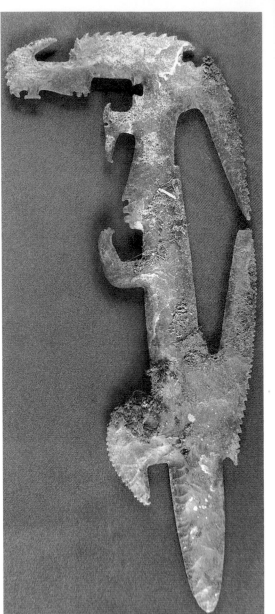

Rosalila Structure Cache

53–57 The objects found in this cache on the floor of the west room of the structure all had strong symbolic connotations and represent one of the finest offerings ever discovered at Copán. Particularly remarkable was the craftspersonship of the eccentric points. (Opposite, above left and right) Eccentric flints, heights 33 cm and 43 cm respectively. (Above and right) Eccentric flints, heights 33 cm and 52 cm. (Opposite, below) A lanceolate flint point, length 35 cm.

Copán Valley, may have served as a line-of-sight in a communications system for relaying fire or smoke signals to the Principal Group.[17] This conceivably had defensive functions, just as we believe the site of Cerro de las Mesas also served for defense.

In this context, we should consider one of the remarkable epigraphic discoveries of David Stuart. Carved in the center of Altar L at Quiriguá is a personage shown seated cross-legged. The name of the protagonist in the accompanying hieroglyphic text ends with the Quiriguá emblem-glyph. The figure itself forms the *ahau* (lord) within the day-sign cartouche, making this one of the most elaborate *ahau* altars on record. Although the coefficient of the *ahau* date is not preserved on the upper part of the altar, '12 Ahau' is cited on the text on the right rim of the altar. The Period Ending date 9.11.0.0.0 fell on the date '12 Ahau 8 Ceh', and given that this was Smoke Imix's great date (similar to what 9.0.0.0.0 had been for Yax K'uk Mo'), it seems likely that the coefficient of the large *ahau* glyph on Altar L was also 12. Smoke Imix God K is himself cited in the rim text, in association with the '12 Ahau 8 Ceh' Period Ending date. The other Calendar Round date on the altar, '9 Chuen 14 Zec', fell on a date 231 days after the great Period Ending, and corresponds to the date of the carving or commemoration of the altar itself, or both. This may have been the date of the accession of the new Quiriguá governor, possibly under the aegis or direct patronage of Smoke Imix God K.

When he discovered that Altar L contains a portrait and the name of Smoke Imix God K, Stuart immediately posed the question: does this mean that Smoke Imix God K had hegemony over Quiriguá? Some have countered that Quiriguá Altar L may simply record a royal visit to Quiriguá on Smoke Imix God K's part, such as documented for rulers at other Classic-period centers. However, the historical record at Quiriguá suggests that the site was, indeed, under the hegemony of Copán, during the reign of the 3rd and 4th rulers. Furthermore, Cauac Sky, the ruler who followed the Altar L individual on the Quiriguá throne, states that he acceded to power *u cab* ('in the land of', or 'in the domain of') the succeeding Copán ruler, 18 Rabbit. Subsequent Quiriguá rulers even claim descent from the Copán founder, Yax K'uk Mo', and cite the same early dates (9.0.0.0.0 and 8.19.15.0.5) as those mentioned in association with Yax K'uk Mo's name on the top of Copán Altar Q. Finally, the 16th Copán ruler, Yax Pac, performs a hand-scattering rite at Quiriguá on the date 9.19.0.0.0, which was recorded on the Quiriguá Acropolis Structure 1-B-1. Thus it seems likely that Smoke Imix God K was more than merely a friendly neighbor to the individual portrayed on Quiriguá Altar L.

After the erection of the six stelae in the valley and Principal Group, Smoke Imix God K still apparently had a lot to say. In the remaining 42 years of his reign, he dedicated Stelae 1, 5, 6, and I, and Altars H', I', and K. Our ongoing investigations of the earlier, now-buried, Acropolis structures will in all likelihood uncover several buildings dating to his reign. One possibility is buried inside Structure 10L-26, and has been given the field name 'Chorcha'.

59 Altar L of Quiriguá. The individual in the cartouche represents the newly-inaugurated ruler of Quiriguá, identified by the name phrase and Quiriguá emblem-glyph to the right of the figure. His inauguration was overseen by Smoke Imix God K, whose name appears in the bottom three glyphs on the left of the figure, following a Period Ending statement.

58 Stela 2, portrait of Smoke Imix God K on the day of his most celebrated Period Ending: 9.11.0.0.0 (AD 652).

60 Copán Stela 6, one of Smoke Imix God K's last monuments, replete with Jaguar Tlaloc imagery. Tlaloc heads emerge from the mouths of the serpent heads on the ceremonial bar, and appear three times in the headdress, along with the 'year-sign' motif.

61–64 The size and contents of Burial XXXVII-4 make this the richest tomb to be uncovered at Copán, and point to the high status enjoyed by its owner. (Left) Interior of the tomb, with the scribe's jade necklace visible in the foreground. The steps which had originally provided access at the back of the tomb chamber were walled up when the chamber was sealed. (Opposite, above left) Copador polychrome vessel found in the tomb, showing a scribe with a diagnostic net cap (see ill. 76), and complete with a paintbrush. This, the paint pots and the probable bark paper book found, point to the conclusion that this was the tomb of a scribe. (Opposite, above right) Ceramic effigy figure from the offerings outside the tomb. Such figures adorn the lids of a number of cylindrical censer vessels which contained ashes. Height of tallest lid 75 cm. (Opposite, below) Fragments of the ceramic effigy lids which had been ritually smashed or 'killed' prior to the burial of the entire tomb chamber.

The platform of Chorcha obscured Mascarón and Papagayo Structures, and it is likely that Smoke Imix God K was the one responsible for this destruction, and the ritual 'killing' and burial of Stela 63, Cu Ix's hieroglyphic step, and of the macaw head ballcourt markers. The building atop the platform measured 30.5 m north–south by 6 m east–west, and was of a very unusual form. This was a large, gallery-like structure with 8 columns framing 7 doorways on both the front and back of the building. Inside this structure was the richest burial ever uncovered in the history of Copán archaeology.[18]

Designated Burial XXXVII-4, this individual was given the benefit of an elaborate, vaulted, masonry tomb, excavated into the sub-flooring of Chorcha.

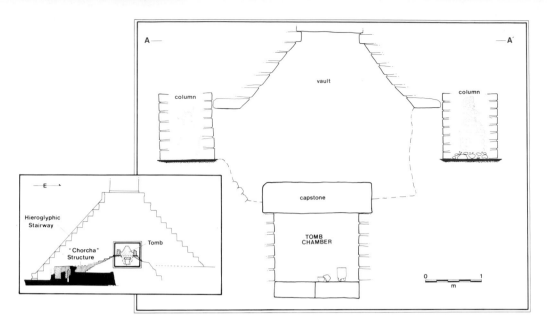

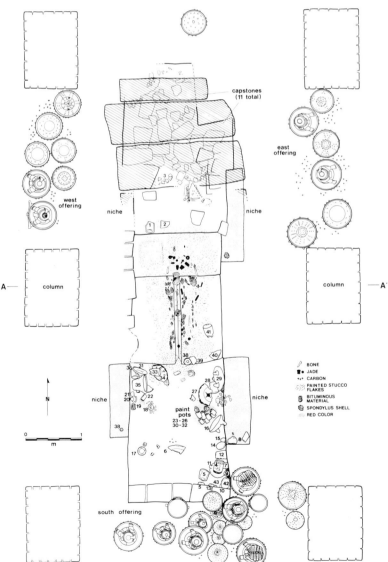

65, 66 *Plan and section of Burial XXXVII-4's tomb chamber, showing the location of the niches and offerings.*

VI (Opposite) *Ceramic effigy figures from the offerings outside the tomb of the Royal Scribe. These figures adorn the lids of a number of cylindrical censer vessels which contained ashes.*

The very large (folio-volume?) and now sadly decayed codex placed next to his head, the 10 paint pots placed in a niche next to his feet and a particularly prized 'Copador' polychrome vessel (see below) with the portrait of a scribe (complete with a paintbrush in the headdress, symbol of the scribal profession) all indicate that this was a man of letters. Laid to rest on (or possibly wrapped in) a sedge mat atop three huge stone slabs, he was wearing a spectacular necklace of polished and carved jades, and his costume contained 19 large spiny oyster shells. Inside the tomb chamber were 44 ceramic vessels, one plaster-coated and painted wooden bowl, numerous other perishable objects also coated with painted plaster, and the remains of a 12-year-old boy. The analysis of the child burial by Rebecca Storey revealed the presence of enamel hypoplasias on his teeth, evidence of malnutrition in the formative years of his life. Storey believes that the child was a member of the lower class sacrificed to accompany this dignitary in the afterlife. Sealing the entrance to the tomb on its south side was a spectacular cache of ceramic incense burners, including seven whose lids were adorned with elaborate half-scale human figures.

The variety, wealth, and sophistication of the offerings in the grave, and its placement in one of the most prominent structures at the site, suggest that this individual was an intimate of the king. The stratigraphic position of the building in which the tomb was built shows that he was buried during the reign of either the 12th or the 13th ruler of Copán. Storey identified the skeletal remains as those of an individual aged 35–40 years, much too young to be either 18 Rabbit (aged more than 60 at death), or Smoke Imix God K (aged more than 80 at death).

Writing in the 16th century, the Fray Diego de Landa wrote that the second sons of rulers were often inducted into the priesthood, if they showed an avocation for the profession. Perhaps the Copán royal scribe was a second son of Smoke Imix God K or 18 Rabbit, one who died before his father (or his brother), and never acceded to the Copán throne.

During the reign of Smoke Imix God K, the valley population continued to grow at an accelerating pace. Smoke Imix God K's reign is correlated with a 'terminal facet' of the Acbi phase, which has distinctive types and proportions of ceramics that characterize the transition from the Middle Classic Acbi phase to the Late Classic Coner phase. Ceramics from this terminal facet of the Acbi phase were found in virtually all valley test-pits where 'pre-Coner' ceramics (see below) were recovered. Occupations had by this time expanded out of the eastern half of the Copán pocket, and evidence of land-use is found in all physiographic zones within the pocket. There is also evidence of occupations dating to this time period outside the pocket proper, including the site of Río Amarillo. The latter half of his reign corresponds with the beginning of the 'Coner phase', which no one would dispute was a time of considerable population increase. My own estimation of the population in the Copán pocket at the end of his reign (in AD 695) is in the order of 8000–12,000 people.

VII *Stela M and the Hieroglyphic Stairway of Structure 10L-26, as reconstructed by Tatiana Proskouriakoff in this watercolor of the 1930s.*

Although we do not yet have adequate samples of the housing, burial practices, and activities of the supporting population from the entire valley, my prediction is that these remains would show a marked tendency towards social stratification.

The evidence suggests that the 67 years of Smoke Imix God K's reign were a dynamic period in the history of the Copán kingdom, including consolidation of the local domain and continued hegemony over the site of Quiriguá and the immediately surrounding area of the Lower Motagua Valley. While the evidence acquired from valley test-pits thus far does not provide irrefutable evidence for a population of 10,000 people, I believe that Copán was certainly in the process of attaining the population size and socio-political complexity associated in most people's minds with statehood, during the reign of Smoke Imix God K. There is little question but that the more remains we uncover and understand from this time period, the more we will respect the achievements of Copán during his time at the helm.

18 Rabbit – statesman and monarch

The 13th ruler in the dynasty of Yax K'uk Mo' was named *Uaxac Lahun Ubac C'awil*, and is referred to by modern scholars as 'XVIII Jog' or '18 Rabbit'. He

67 Stela J, with the mat-weave on the east side (facing the Maya road or sacbe *coming in from Las Sepulturas) carrying an inscription citing the first Period Ending after the accession to power of 18 Rabbit. The text also recalls the famed 9.0.0.0.0 Period Ending rite and the name of the founder, Yax K'uk Mo'.*

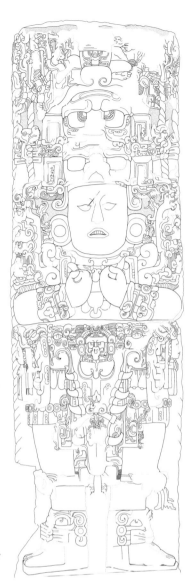

68 *Stela C, east side: portrait of 18 Rabbit as a young man. Note the crocodile head on his belt, complete with dangling front limbs.*

acceded to the throne 21 days after the death of Smoke Imix God K, on 9 July AD 695. He reigned for 43 years, the third-longest reign in the history of the city, but his actual birth-date is as yet unknown. Although 18 Rabbit followed the tradition of erecting numerous stelae, he altered the patterns of his predecessor. Unlike the widely-distributed stelae of Smoke Imix God K, 18 Rabbit's stelae are all found in the Principal Group, and all but one of them (Stela J) were erected in the Great Plaza. After his earliest, low-relief stela (his accession monument, Stela J), 18 Rabbit also distinguished himself by the exceedingly high relief of his portraits, some of which are nearly full-round. Likewise, the sculptures which he had carved on the final version of Structure 22 are carved in very high-relief, and in a fluid and naturalistic style. It can be said that art under the reign of this ruler reached its greatest level of aesthetic and technical sophistication in the history of the city.

In addition to erecting the stelae in the Great Plaza, 18 Rabbit also erected the steps or 'bleachers' on the east, west, and north sides of the Great Plaza, and the final versions of Structures 10L-2 and 10L-4. It is possible to conclude on the basis of style and depth of relief that he also built Structures 10L-20 and 10L-21 of the East Court, as well as an early version of Structure 10L-22A, the penultimate version of Structure 10L-26, and the final version of the main ballcourt (Ballcourt A-III).[19] The three playing-alley floor markers of Ballcourt A-IIb represent a particularly fine set of monuments, placed in that court by 18 Rabbit as his stamp upon the ballfield created by his ancestors, before he built his own, much more imposing, version.

Copán's population was by this time growing as never before; the Copán polychrome ware known as Copador was being manufactured and distributed; and on Stela A the ruler claims to have either some sort of equivalence to, or association with, three other major centers – Tikal, Site 'Q' (thought to be Calakmul by most scholars), and Palenque – or to have been visited by the lords of those places during the commemoration of the stela. Copán may have controlled the valleys to the north and east as far away as Quiriguá and the La Venta Valley, respectively, and there is evidence within the Copán pocket for an increasingly status-conscious display of stone sculptures at Structure 9N-82 C 2nd of Group 9N-8. 18 Rabbit's domain was a vast and complex one. To judge from his monuments and the rapid growth of his city he was skilled at both statecraft and the staging of rituals.

69 Playing alley markers of Ballcourt AIIb. The central marker shows 18 Rabbit (on the left) squaring off with the God of Number 0, one of the gods of the Underworld.

CHAPTER SIX

THE COPÁN MOSAIC: RECONSTRUCTING ARCHITECTURE, RELIGION, AND HISTORY

As if jealous of this superb creation of man, all the most violent forces of nature seem to have conspired to destroy it. Even in historic times, earthquakes have shaken the ruins, and now the beautifully carved fragments of its buildings lie scattered on the slopes of its pyramids like the pieces of a gigantic jigsaw puzzle in stone.[1]

The architectural sculpture of Copán

Over the centuries, the rulers developed a religious ideology which assigned and perpetuated their supernatural authority. By promoting a world order that explained both the cosmos and the divine right of the Copán rulers, the centralized authority sought to achieve consensus and to reinforce their political and economic power over the inhabitants of the valley. As time passed, the reinforcement of status through the erection of sculpture and architectural monuments spread from the Principal Group to the aspiring nobility residing in the valley. Besides the purely religious or political monuments erected by the kings in the Principal Group, it seems that virtually everyone of the Copán upper class was obsessed with documenting their station in life. In sculptures adorning buildings, the landed aristocracy displayed their supernatural patrons and secular authority, their personal history and genealogy, and their relations with the Copán royal house. Unfortunately, the constituent materials of Copán buildings did not stand the test of time well.

Lime plaster was reserved for sealing the floors, terraces, and roofs of the buildings, and periodic 'white-washings' (often in dazzling colors) were used to seal and protect the buildings from rainwater. Once the structures were abandoned, the lime plaster cracked, water and plants penetrated the fills, and earthquakes toppled weakened structures. Soon the tropical forest returned.

There is also evidence that some structures were deliberately destroyed or pilfered in the years following the collapse of the Copán dynasty. Each new excavation of a sculpture-adorned building provides more evidence for the degree to which the post-dynastic peoples moved and removed sculptures. Consistently, the pieces missing in greatest numbers from buildings are the human and deity heads, hands, and hieroglyphic fragments, all apparently of interest to the squatters and collectors who have altered the site over the centuries. Unintentionally, the 19th- and early 20th-century archaeologists themselves subsequently contributed to the confusion by stacking up the fallen façade sculptures from numerous buildings in piles scattered around the site. Since locations for the individual pieces were not recorded, and the wild variety of the mosaic fragments themselves did nothing to facilitate their reconstruction, no concerted effort toward studying this unprecedented corpus of art had been undertaken since the Carnegie expeditions. The present work at the site has succeeded in confirming many details of Proskouriakoff's reconstructions, at the same time enabling us to see and understand things that simply were not possible in her day.

The Copán Mosaics Project is dedicated to collaboration with the Instituto Hondureño de Antropología e Historia in the conservation, study, and, where possible, re-articulation and interpretation of the more than 25,000 fragments of sculpture lying about the surface of the Acropolis and Great Plaza of the site core, and in the storage facilities of the Instituto. This has involved the location and cleaning of the sculptures themselves, their study and documentation in a formal catalog, construction of new storage and laboratory facilities for the long-term conservation and analysis of the material, and the interpretation of the sculptures which can be securely associated with a particular building. Conceived and begun as a rescue operation, the project has developed into a long-term study of the fallen sculptures, including the reconstruction of the architecture, religion, and history of ancient Copán. (The formal catalog alone includes descriptions, scale drawings, photographs, assigning of provenience where possible, restoration of broken pieces, and re-articulation of adjacent blocks.)

Theory and method of analysis

Using archaeological evidence of the 8th- and 9th-century public monuments of the Principal Group, and from the entire valley, our goals are to unravel the forms and nature of ideological and political adaptations developed by Copán's central authority for confronting the social and political problems documented in the archaeology of the valley, as well as the historical records carved in stone in the Principal Group.

Our strategy is to document historical events first, and then to reconstruct and interpret religious and political imagery. The inscriptions and architectural stratigraphy allow us to date particular events, including those of the construction and subsequent modification of the major monuments of the site core. The decipherment of public records on inscribed stone monuments gives us some knowledge of the historical events considered important enough to be recorded by those in power. Rigorous analyses of the components of the building façades allow us to reconstruct their original forms and to interpret their meanings as the art and architectural centerpiece of the Copán kingdom.

70 *Sculpture Pile 5, located east of Ballcourt A-III, as it appeared at the onset of the Copán Mosaics Project. The fragments from this pile are now known to derive from seven different structures.*

Ultimately we hope to be able to describe and interpret ancient Maya statecraft at Copán, using both documentary and archaeological evidence. Our evaluation of the veracity and significance of the public monuments incorporates a healthy dose of skepticism from the social scientists on and outside the project.

Reconstruction of the historical record is based on the accurate dating of buildings through hieroglyphic decipherment and interpretation of architectural stratigraphy. In some cases we can use the records of earlier expeditions to match and reconstruct the scattered sculptural fragments. However, when we began the project, only a few hundred of the more than 25,000 mosaic fragments could be assigned to their original façades. We soon realized nevertheless that each façade was distinctive even if general styles were similar. Therefore by carefully digging untouched parts of a specific structure, we can obtain samples of mosaic sculpture obviously fallen from that building. This information allows us to determine which motifs adorned the structure in question, and helps us to cull other examples of those motifs – carved in the same size, style, and depth of relief – from the unprovenanced fragments. The fact that most of the façade stones were carved in place on the structure enables us to re-articulate many fragments from the same building.

We have followed this procedure in the excavation of the four sides of the pyramidal substructure of the Hieroglyphic Stairway, and in the investigation of all the extant buildings in the East Court of the Acropolis. These methods have proven so successful that the work has been expanded accordingly.

House of the Bacabs

71 (Above) *Structure 9N-82 C 1st (the 'House of the Bacabs'), as restored by Rudy Larios.*

72 (Left) *A scribal patron emerging from the east niche on the front façade of Structure 9N-82 C 1st, as restored by Rudy Larios. Note the sectioned conch shell inkpot, held in the left hand.*

73 (Right, above) *Reconstruction of the front (north) façade of Structure 9N-82 C 1st, based on the architectural studies of Rudy Larios and the sandbox work of the author.*

74 (Right) *Burial VIII-6, found in association with Structure 9N-82 C 2nd. Note the jade bar pectoral placed over the chest.*

75 (Far right) *The central figure of the front façade of Structure 9N-82 C 1st, as reconstructed in the sandbox. Note the depiction of a jade bar pectoral on the chest (see ill. 73).*

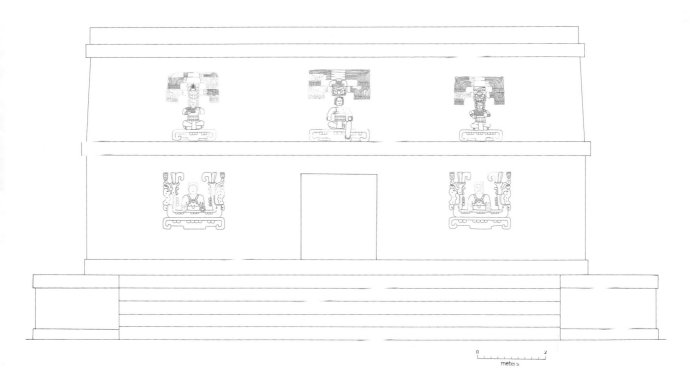

These reconstructions tell us much about ancient Maya religion, history, social structure, and political organization at Copán. Some of the most fascinating results are those which bear upon the relationship between the rulers in the Principal Group and their subjects in the valley. To illustrate this let us examine the building which inspired us to undertake the Copán Mosaics Project: Sepulturas Structure 9N-82 ('House of the Bacabs').[2]

The lower part of the front façade of Structure 9N-82 contained the busts of two anthropomorphic figures emerging from serpent jaws. The better preserved figure carries a sectioned conch-shell inkpot in his left hand. Buried in the fill of this final version of the building were the fragments of a similar figure used in the preceding version of the structure, the earlier figure having been carved in the round. In addition to the conch-shell inkpot, the earlier figure carries a paintbrush in its right hand. Finally its 'monkey-man' face and 'extra' deer ear identify it as a Classic Maya scribe.[3]

The association of these two figures with successive constructions of the building suggest that the office of scribe was passed from father to son. The grave of a scribe (Burial VIII-6) was found below the northeast corner of the building where he revered the statue of his supernatural patron. On his chest was found a jadeite bar pectoral identical in size and treatment to the one carved on the figure placed above the central doorway of the final structure, dated to the reign of the 16th ruler, Yax Pac. The protagonist of the associated bench inscription is either his father, or himself wearing the same bar pectoral status symbol as his father. This and other epigraphic and iconographic evidence from the bench reinforce the interpretation that the scribal office was an inherited one by this time, as it was at the time of the Spanish conquest and recorded in legal documents and court cases from Yucatán documented and analyzed by Ralph Roys in his book *The Titles of Ebtun*. Finally, new readings of the inscription on the bench and of the reused texts incorporated in its steps show that the Structure 9N-82 scribes commemorated their strong affiliations with the rulers Smoke Imix, 18 Rabbit, and Yax Pac.[4]

In his book, *The Maya Scribe and His World*, Michael Coe has argued that scribes were held in great esteem among the Classic Maya, just as they were among the later Mexica (Aztecs). The Spanish priest Pedro de Sahagun said the Mexica conceived of scribes in this way: 'The good scribe is honest, circumspect, far-sighted, pensive; a judge of colors, an applier of the colors, who makes shadows, forms feet, face, hair. He paints, applies color, makes shadows, draws gardens, paints flowers, creates works of art'. Coe concluded that the scribal profession was restricted to élite noble lines, as suggested both by the Mexica and evidence from 16th-century Yucatán. He further surmised that only members of élite lineages in Classic Maya society had any chance of escaping the Underworld after death, as did the Hero Twins in their epic battle

76 (Opposite) The 'Monkey Man' patron of Maya scribes and artists, from Structure 9N-82 C 1st. The simian facial features, and 'extra' deer ear above his ear identify this deity. Note the sectioned conch shell inkpot held in the left hand, and the paintbrush held in the right. Height 52 cm.

with the Lords of the Underworld in the *Popol Vuh*. The façade and bench of Structure 9N-82, and the burial and statue associated with this building, provide solid archaeological evidence for Coe's arguments. The requisite noble status and, hence, exclusivity of scribes, and the skills and wisdom attributed to these individuals, securely places them in the upper echelon of Copán society. These were men of great prestige, who quite likely wielded considerable power as well.

The monuments of 18 Rabbit

As we have seen, the steps of the final version of the House of the Bacabs incorporate reused fragments with hieroglyphs. These cite the death of Smoke Imix God K, and an anniversary of the accession to power of the 13th ruler, 18 Rabbit. The epigrapher David Stuart has shown that this accession anniversary was also cited in the inscribed step of the inner chamber of Structure 10L-22, long considered the single most beautiful building at Copán. The inner chamber of Structure 10L-22 contains a cosmogram of the Maya world, showing the levels of the Underworld – represented by skulls of the buried ancestors; of the middle world, where mortals reside – seated upon the surface of which were the sky-bearers (*Bacabs*), whose charge it was to support the sky; and of the heavens – represented by a two-headed sky serpent, in whose intertwined body dance the gods themselves.

Art historians Mary Miller and Linda Schele believe that the rulers – beginning with 18 Rabbit – performed auto-sacrificial bloodletting rituals in the inner chamber of Structure 10L-22, in order to commune with their ancestors and with the gods depicted in the archway over the entrance to the chamber.[5] This hypothesis is supported by the discovery that the large stone masks decorating the four exterior corners of the building are not rain gods (*Chacs*), as previously supposed, but were glyphically labeled by the Maya as *tun witz* (stone mountain). Therefore, Structure 10L-22 can be interpreted to represent a man-made 'sacred mountain', such as those used by the modern Maya during religious pilgrimages for communion with their ancestors. The culmination of the modern pilgrimage comes when incense and candles are burned at the sacred crosses at the mouths of caves, where the ancestors are thought to reside. In the case of Structure 10L-22, the entrance to the building was carved with the image of a giant earth deity – representing the mouth of the cave in the sacred mountain – and the inner chamber would have represented the sacred recesses where communion with the ancestral deities was sought. The façade of Structure 10L-22 was also replete with images of the maize god, sprouting from stony mountain symbols (*tun witz*), indicating that fertility was a main concern of the rulers' intercessions with the gods.

The Maya practice of auto-sacrificial rituals involving bloodletting, and the sacrifice of animals and even humans, was carefully documented by Spanish

77 (Left) The inner chamber of Structure 10L-22, representing a cosmogram. The skulls on the lower level represent the Underworld, where the dead reside. The sky-bearers or bacabs of the east and west are shown seated atop the skulls, in the surface world where mortals reside. The bacabs support the two-headed saurian deity whose body represents the sky, in which are intertwined the gods and ancestral deities brought forth by the king's rituals. When standing or seated in the doorway, the ruler was symbolically placed at the center of the Maya cosmos.

78 (Right) Corner masks from Structure 10L-22, as restored by the Copán Mosaics Project. The masks carry tun (stone) and witz (mountain or hill) signs, labeling the building as a sacred stone mountain.

79 *Sculpture Pile 2, containing fragments removed from the Carnegie excavations of Ballcourt A-III, as it appeared at the onset of the Copán Mosaics Project. Structure 10L-10 of the ballcourt is visible in the background.*

priests during the 16th and 17th centuries but long dismissed by 20th-century Mayanists as an 'aberration' introduced to Yucatán by 'invading Mexicans' during the Early Postclassic period. More recently, however, new analyses of Classic Maya pictorial sculpture and hieroglyphic writing by David Joralemon, David Stuart, Linda Schele and Mary Miller have shown that bloodletting in auto-sacrificial rituals was an important ceremony performed by Maya rulers. Indeed, the 'scattering' verb so common in Classic Maya inscriptions (see illus. 17 and 18) is interpreted by most authorities as the letting of blood by the ruler himself. These 'scattering' rituals were performed at most major Period Endings, that is, at the completion of every 5 *tuns* (5 × 360 days) in the Long Count. It is possible that the blood, indeed the lives, of other people, and certainly of animals such as deer, jaguars, and turkey, were also offered at these and other special occasions, since evidence for such practices exists in Maya art, bark-paper books, and even in some cases (see Chapter Eight) in the archaeological record.

The sacred, as opposed to martial, symbolism of Structure 10L-22 has parallels in many other monuments commemorated during the reign of 18 Rabbit. In particular, the stelae of the Great Plaza emphasize the themes of fertility, solar worship, and other realms of Classic Maya religion, and this has led Claude Baudez to point out that 18 Rabbit was concerned with more than just conquest. He was an extremely active ruler, responsible for building the steps of the Great Plaza, and the erection of its seven stelae (A, B, C, D, F, H, and 4); for the final versions of the buildings defining the north and south sides of the Great Plaza (Structures 10L-2 and 10L-4); for alterations to the penultimate Ballcourt A-IIb and the construction of the final Ballcourt A-III; and for part or all of the penultimate versions of Structures 10L-26, 10L-22, and – judging from the style of their sculptures – 10L-20 and 10L-21. Indeed, Linda Schele believes that 18 Rabbit was the greatest single patron of the arts in Copán's history, based on the number of his works and on the contribution of an extremely naturalistic, fluid, high-relief style of carving.

Besides Structure 10L-22, the best-known and preserved architectural monument of 18 Rabbit's reign is the final Ballcourt A-III. It is a very large and imposing edifice, in size second only to the Great Court at Chichén Itzá. Ballcourt A-III is certainly one of the most elaborately embellished of its kind ever created, with sculpture decorating the floor of the playing alley where the players moved about, the inclined benches upon which the ball was bounced, and in profusion on the four façades of the two temples built up and away from the field of play.

The now badly-eroded markers on the floor of the playing alley originally showed scenes where players were portrayed with the large rubber ball used in the game. The inclined benches each had a raised surface running transversely through their central axes, inscribed with hieroglyphic text. The inscription

80 Structure 10L-10 of Ballcourt A-III, showing the scarlet macaw as conceived by Barbara Fash and restored by Rudy Larios of the Copán Mosaics Project in 1988. This 'composite reconstruction' combines the best preserved examples of the different motifs (claws, serpent wings, tail feathers, etc.).

cites the commemoration date of the building (9.15.6.8.13 10 Ben 16 Kayab, or 10 January AD 738), a few months before the death of this distinguished ruler. At the tops of the benches there were vertically-tenoned macaw heads, one along the central axis and one at each end of both buildings. These are also called 'markers', though their actual function during the game is not yet resolved. Earlier versions of the ballcourt also had playing-alley floor markers and vertically-tenoned macaw-head bench markers, indicating a continuity in decoration during the ballcourt's *c.* 400 years of use.

The Copán Mosaics Project began its work in 1985 with the task of re-articulating, conserving, and studying the mosaic sculptures of Ballcourt A-III. The façade fragments were excavated by Derek Nusbaum and Gustav Stromsvik of the Carnegie Institution and carefully stacked in four discrete piles in the immediate confines of the ballcourt. There were more than 1200 ballcourt pieces, falling into a series of discrete motif categories: scarlet macaw body parts, feathered collars, *akbal* (darkness) signs, maize and vegetation, and vertically-tenoned 'bony *ahau*' pieces.

After calculating the minimum number of individual figures, and much patient experimenting and re-evaluating, Barbara Fash devised reconstructions for 16 ballcourt birds. Work with the wedge-shaped tenons of the pieces demonstrated to her that four of the birds on each building were placed on the corners, thus leaving the other four to be placed on the columns between the doorways on the east and west sides of each of the two structures. The birds are each composed of a head with open beak surrounded by a beaded collar, left and right talons placed below the collar, wings – complete with the serpent-head symbol that is placed on bird wings in Maya art – which extend horizontally from the sides of the collar and body, an elaborate tail assemblage including the *akbal* symbol, and a cascade of tail feathers bifurcating and then extending symmetrically in two courses to the left and right of the central tail assemblage. (A composite example combining the best-preserved examples of all these motifs into a single bird has been restored and placed on the eastern structure of the ballcourt, facing the playing alley, so that the visitor to Copán can get an idea of how the sculptured façade looked in its original state.)

Studies of the accounts in the *Popol Vuh* (the Sacred Book of the 17th-century Quiché Maya) and of the surviving bark-paper books show that the macaw was a symbol for the sun. Since the Ballcourt A-III macaws all carry *akbal* signs on their tails, perhaps the metaphor here is that the birds represent the sun in the Underworld, combating the forces of darkness and death. As we saw in the previous chapter, it has long been thought that the main religious connotations of the Mesoamerican ballgame were the perpetuation of natural cycles such as the movements of the sun and of other celestial bodies, and of the

VIII *Jade figurine of a man from the Hieroglyphic Stairway cache, representing the finest example of its kind yet discovered at Copán. Height 14 cm.*

IX *Jade figurine of the patron of war.*

transition of the seasons and of fertility. At Copán, the vegetation scrolls found on the roof drains of the ballcourt, and the maize vegetation motif repeated 32 times on the façades of the two buildings, clearly refer to the fertility cult. When the king or his representatives defeated the forces of disease, drought, and death – symbolized in the costumes of the members of the opposing team – he succeeded in ensuring that the sun would once again rise triumphant in the east and that the rains would be plentiful and arrive on time.

There is abundant evidence from other Classic Maya sites that losers in the ballgame were sacrificed, and it is entirely possible that in his day 18 Rabbit himself dispatched a few vanquished players.

On one altar, and on a small stone cylinder now on display in the Copán Museum, 18 Rabbit also cites the captures made in war against some smaller sites in the region. Indeed, Linda Schele believes that he was in pursuit of captives for the dedication of his new ballcourt when he was himself captured, and subsequently beheaded on 3 May AD 738 by the ruler Cauac Sky from the site of Quiriguá. The question of how this long-lived and distinguished Copán dynast was killed by a rival from a much smaller kingdom has perplexed scholars for some time. What is certain is that this was a seminal event in the history of both sites, as we will see.

The high-relief, rounded, and very naturalistic style championed by 18 Rabbit on his stelae, on Structure 10L-22, and on the final phase ballcourt, are also in evidence on the façade sculptures which decorated Structures 10L-20 and 10L-21 of the East Court. The research in the East Court of the Acropolis, directed by Robert Sharer, may yet obtain stratigraphic evidence that will help in the determination of whether or not these two large structures were contemporary with Structure 10L-22.

The named buildings or 'houses' of the Acropolis

Structure 10L-20, now completely destroyed by the ravages of the Copán River, once displayed an ominously decorated façade. Members of the Peabody Museum and Carnegie Institution expeditions record that a series of large sculptures of Killer Bats adorned the exterior of the building. The bats were identified by the death signs (%) on their pectorals, and their 'death eye' collars, as the same grisly Underworld denizens described in the *Popol Vuh*. More recently, we have collected all the surviving fragments of these bats from the Acropolis and the local museum and storage facilities, and calculated that there were at least six of these Killer Bats.

X *Reconstruction of a jaguar sacrifice at Altar Q, during the reign of Yax Pac. Attendants dress as aspects of Chac, the god of rain and lightning, while central figures are attired like the royal ancestors shown on Altar Q. Painting by Tom Hall, courtesy of the National Geographic Society.*

Structure 10L-20 had been described by Palacio in the 16th century as a 'tower', and before its destruction by the river at the turn of this century it was partially excavated by Maudslay. His excavations revealed that the super-structure had two floors, and that the building's cord-holders (for securing the doors) were set on the outside. This placement was taken to indicate that the building was designed to be sealed from the outside, and led the Austrian architects Hasso Hohmann and Annegrette Vogrin to conclude that Structure 10L-20 was a jail. Its adornment with Killer Bats, its similarity to the 'House of Bats' described in the *Popol Vuh*, and the Lacandon Maya custom of confining prospective victims of sacrificial rites in wooden cages all strengthen this interpretation. In the Lacandon case, guards slept on top to prevent the escape of the prisoners. The Killer Bat sculptures, as noted by Proskouriakoff in *An Album of Maya Architecture*, were roof ornaments.

The *Popol Vuh* also names other 'Houses of Torture'. If Structure 10L-20 represents a Classic period version of the House of Bats, do other such named houses exist at Copán or at other Classic Period sites? One possibility is Structure 10L-21, immediately north of Structure 10L-20, and also a tall, prominent edifice in the Late Classic East Court. Barbara Fash and the author have suggested elsewhere that Structure 10L-21 may represent the *chayim ha*: 'House of Knives' or 'Razor House'.[6] The general meaning of *chay* is obsidian, and a more general interpretation may be simply 'obsidian house'.

Structure 10L-21 is decorated with some rather ominous motifs, one of which appears to be an eccentric knife, with cross-hatching to indicate a black stone, that is, obsidian. More intriguing, however, is the motif of interwoven eyes running around all four sides of this structure. The eyes have gouged-out pupils, and an intact example excavated by Julie Miller at Structure 10L-21, shows that they were filled with obsidian disks. The Tlaloc heads adorning the building also have gouged-out pupils, presumably also for obsidian inlays. This evidence of the prominence of obsidian and sacrifice clearly make Structure 10L-21 an excellent candidate for the *chayim ha*.

Further evidence for a named house in the East Court of Copán has been found at Structure 10L-22A, built on to the west side of Structure 10L-22. Long known to have a *pop* (mat) design on its façade, this building has gone largely unnoticed since its initial exploration by the Carnegie expeditions. In 1988 we set out to test Barbara Fash's hypothesis that this building represented the *popol na* – the Mat House or 'Community House' cited in the 16th-century Maya Motul dictionary. Project epigrapher Nikolai Grube has discovered that such houses still exist in traditional Maya communities in Quintana Roo.[7] Our excavation of Structure 10L-22A uncovered sculpture fragments comprising 10 mat symbols, adorning the lower part of the building. Parts of two examples were *in situ* on the east wall and matched the positions of two fallen examples from the west wall. A collapsed but still-ordered example of the mat fallen in front of the west doorway indicated that there were three mats on the front side of the building (one over each doorway), and three mats on the back.

*81 A Killer Bat from Structure 10L-20, now on display in the Copán Museum. Note the %
(death) sign on the pectoral. Height 75 cm.*

Alternating with the mats on the front and back sides of the building were a
total of 8 human figures, each seated cross-legged over a large hieroglyph. The
hieroglyphs appear to be place-names, possibly the names of once-thriving
communities in the kingdom.[8] Above the figures were a series of glyphs which
read *ahau lil* (governance, or act of governing), a symbol much in keeping with
the proposed function of this edifice.

The anthropologist Ralph Roys, in analyzing 16th-century Maya political
organization in Yucatán, documented an important political office that can
serve as an ethnohistoric analogy. Roys noted that *ah holpop* means 'he who is
at the head of the mat', and the mat was frequently used as the symbol of
government. In his account of Hocaba, one of the large towns in northern
Yucatán at the time of the conquest, the *encomendero* tells us: 'This lord
governed and ruled his people in this province with his cacique [local
chieftains], whom they called holpop, who were like the regidors or captains,
and through these they treated with the lord for what they desired'.[9]

The analogy with the *holpop* and *popol na* of 16th-century Yucatán has
other information in its favor. The Motul dictionary defines the *holpop* as:
'Head of the banquet. Item: The steward, master of the house called popolna,
where they assembled to discuss public affairs and learn to dance for the town
festivals.' The open nature of the front of Structure 10L-22A would make an
appropriate place for meetings of the ruler, his eight 'local chieftains', and

82 *Structure 10L-22A during the 1988 excavations, with the woven mat design found on the east side of Structure 10L-22A visible in the foreground. The interior of the building has been partially cleared.*

83 *Collapsed but still partially articulated mat design fallen directly in front of the west doorway of Structure 10L-22A. Charred fragments of the hardwood Chico Zapote were found on the floor, indicating that the wooden lintel over the doorway had burned, causing the mat design to collapse in front of the door.*

84 *(Below) Large hieroglyphs representing place-names, from Structure 10L-22A (the Mat House).*

  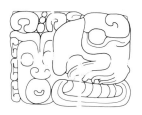 

  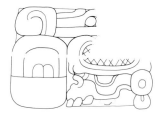

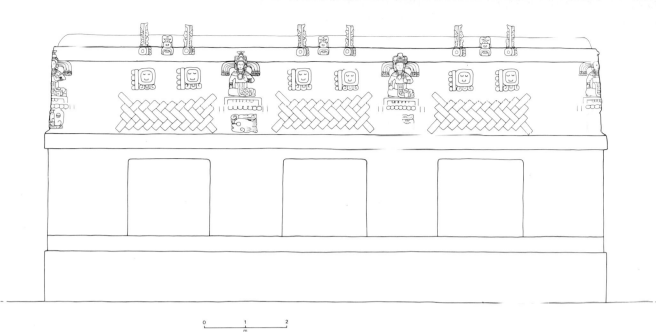

85 *Provisional reconstruction drawing of the south (front) façade of Structure 10L-22A, based on collaborations between Barbara Fash and Rudy Larios.*

86 *Structure 10L-22A, the* popol na *(Mat House), as restored by the Copán Acropolis Archaeological Project in 1990. Restoration of the mat sculptures was based on the position and form of the example still* in situ *on the east side of the building, and the position and form of the example found in front of the west doorway (see ill. 82).*

other close confidants. The presence of a midden found in excavations at the southwest corner of the building also suggests that 'banquets' could indeed have been prepared there. Admittedly, the size and the floor plan of Structure 10L-22A do not seem appropriate as a dance floor, but even in this there is structural evidence that supports the 16th-century analogy: an elevated masonry platform (Structure 10L-25) measuring some 35 m north–south by 8.5 m east–west, was built directly in front of Structure 10L-22A. The size of the platform, and its lack of dividers, or of any kind of building walls on its summit, certainly conform to what one would expect for a dance platform.

The best clues to the identity of the valley statesmen portrayed on Structure 10L-22A are the glyphs that identify their place of origin, and the distinctive collar and headdress elements that they wear. The collar and headdress icons may represent the trades or special products for which the different divisions were known. In this context it bears noting that the epigrapher Peter Mathews recognized that the glyph under another one of the figures is the same as a location cited in the text of Stela 10, on the western limits of the Copán pocket. Similarly, the bust with the tied-rope pectoral from Structure 10L-22A has an analogue in a bust (possibly an effigy of the representative from that ward) from a building in the large site at the end of the Sepulturas causeway, on the eastern limit of the urban core of ancient Copán. It is also possible that some of the representatives came from major towns beyond the limits of the Copán pocket, such as Río Amarillo, El Paraiso, El Puente, and Los Higos.

The chieftains portrayed on Structure 10L-22A came to the aid of their ruler, and of their kingdom, at one of its darkest hours. The date of the building's dedication, provided by the numerous examples of '9 Ahau' glyphs fallen from the façade – and corroborated by stratigraphic and stylistic evidence – was the Period Ending 9.15.15.0.0 9 Ahau 18 Xul, or 12 June AD 746.[10] This was only eight years after the death of 18 Rabbit at the hands of Cauac Sky of Quiriguá. To have their esteemed god-king captured and beheaded by a ruler whose fiefdom had been subservient to Copán was doubtless a shattering defeat, one that would have shaken confidence in the entire religious and political system. The succeeding ruler Smoke Monkey's apparent response was to draw in his governors and lords to a public meeting house, to portray them prominently on the building's façade, and pay homage to their role in their communities', and their state's, future. Of considerable interest is that Smoke Monkey did not place his own portrait on a stela in front of the building itself. This decentralized approach was later to be greatly over-shadowed by the works of his successors. Indeed, until Structure 10L-22A was dug in 1988, Smoke Monkey and his lords had been relegated to complete obscurity.

Political strategies of the last Copán kings

The refined dating and other historical, political, and religious information provided by the profuse decoration on the buildings of ancient Copán enable us to document particulars of its growth, development, and decline in considerable detail. These data and the hypotheses tested and re-evaluated by them have the further virtue of providing models for institutions and evolutionary processes in other parts of the Maya area, and beyond. Certainly the office of local chieftain or spokesman which we postulate to have been glorified in Smoke Monkey's Structure 10L-22A is one for which there is ample evidence in both Classic and Postclassic times.

The hereditary or non-hereditary nature of the offices held by subsidiary lords and governors, and their duties and perquisites throughout the Maya area are being addressed by both archaeologists and epigraphers.[11] The implications of Structure 10L-22A for the study of Maya statecraft and political evolution are twofold. First, they suggest that governors and subsidiary lords were of sufficient importance to wield strong authority in the fate of large Classic Maya city-states, particularly in political crisis. Second, if one of the fundamental characteristics of statehood is the separation of political institutions from kinship lines, then from AD 746, if not before, Copán was at that stage of development. The statesmen are identified not by their personal names, but rather by the name of the subdivision of the kingdom which they represent. This formal set of jurisdictions and representatives implies that Late Classic Maya political organization at Copán was moving towards more institutionalized forms of government which cut across traditional kinship lines and interests.

At this juncture, it is not possible for us to determine how successful Smoke Monkey's strategy was. The inscriptions tell us only that he died within three years of completing Structure 10L-22A, and was succeeded by the 15th ruler, Smoke Shell. The monumental record indicates that Smoke Shell's strategy was the exact opposite of the decentralized, modest work of Smoke Monkey. Smoke Shell poured all his efforts into the refurbishment of Structure 10L-26, including the world's largest hieroglyphic stairway. The purpose of this monument was to emphasize the glorious days (and rulers) of the kingdom, and in the process lend legitimacy to Smoke Shell himself as the sole inheritor of the supernatural and secular power of the Copán throne. Did he do this because of renewed support from the lords, won at the cost of the prestige of his predecessor? Or was Structure 10L-26 his reaction to the growing power and influence of those formerly subordinate nobles? These are among the new questions which our research has posed, and which are at present not yet resolved.

Copán scribes and warriors

The study of the Copán scribes can tell us as much about Maya society as it does about their own lives and social station. The 5th-century curer or shaman represented in Burial VIII-36 of Las Sepulturas lived nearly a kilometer from the center of Copán, and from the monuments of the founder of the Copán dynasty. Yet he was a man of letters and of considerable economic means, to judge from the codex and other valuable goods he took with him to the afterlife. The evidence from his grave and person suggests that his status was at least as much achieved as ascribed. Was he the first scribe of the lineage later represented by the two scribes, and successive buildings, of Structure 9N-82?

The lives of these later scribes span the time from the death of Smoke Imix God K to the middle of the reign of Yax Pac, the 16th ruler, to judge from the associated inscriptions. Although the earlier version of Structure 9N-82 is more modest – probably more in keeping with what scribes' houses at most other Classic-period sites would look like – the final version is indeed a sumptuous structure. The final scribe, Mac Chaanal, was allowed to carve an inscription which honored not only the reigning king, Yax Pac, but Mac Chaanal's own ancestry, including both his father's and mother's names in the 16-glyph text. This supports the interpretation that Structure 10L-22A does signal a decentralization of power, and that the local nobility were allowed (or perhaps usurped) greater authority than in previous generations.

In this context it is worth noting that even at a site with as clear a record as that of Group 9N-8, there are gaps in the record. For instance, no monument dating to Smoke Monkey's reign has thus far been found. What was the role of this site when the state and its authority were in a time of crisis? Similarly, despite intensive excavations at Group 9N-8, we have no burial which could represent the remains of Mac Chaanal. What became of an individual with such a distinguished palace to call his own? Was he run out of town in a moment of political upheaval? (Alternatively, as suggested long ago by Storey, was he buried in the Principal Group? Such distinction had previously been given to the royal scribe (Burial XXXVII-4), who had more offerings, and the greatest amount of effort and care lavished upon the construction of his funerary chamber, than anyone yet unearthed in 100 years of investigations at Copán.)

At present, warriors are less well-represented in the Copán Valley settlements. While it might be tempting to leap to the conclusion that Copán was a city of scribes and not of warriors, this would be grossly premature. We believe that the reason we have not yet found warriors' quarters is simply the small size of our site sample. As more valley sites with sculpture are excavated, it will be possible to see if hereditary or elected warriors also left records of their office, achievements, and names. (Such a case has been documented at Group 4 in Palenque, on the Tablet of the Slaves, where the governor and war chief (*sahal*, or *cahal*) Chac Zutz cites his martial exploits in considerable detail.)[12]

The king as warrior is certainly a prominent theme in the architectural monuments of the Principal Group from the time of the 15th ruler. But again we have a sampling problem: all the buildings completely excavated and studied so far date to the 8th and 9th centuries. Thus we cannot know yet to what extent warfare was a theme of previous buildings, or rulers. In what we have been able to uncover of the earlier Acropolis buildings, however, it appears that the processes documented in the later monuments all seem to have earlier counterparts.

Nevertheless, given the bellicose nature of the Late Classic Maya political landscape, and the long reign of Smoke Imix God K, it is certainly logical to conclude that Smoke Imix God K must have been an accomplished warrior-king. At the very least, he must have had some fine warriors in his employ. In looking at the records of the rulers themselves, one is struck by the fact that the king whose monuments best stand the test of objective material (and materialist) scrutiny, was probably successful in all three realms considered in this chapter: as scribe, warrior, and statesman. But what of his predecessors?

There is still much to do in both the valley and at the Principal Group, and a great deal to learn about the other Copán rulers, before we can affirm the monumental claims of those men. The study of the Early Acropolis and its many antecedent complexes of buildings by Sharer should do much to illuminate these and other important issues.

Certainly the Copán data serve to demonstrate that it is indeed possible to document the interaction between the Classic period ruler and his supporting population. This was first achieved through the complete excavation of valley sites by Gordon Willey and William Sanders in their respective research projects in Las Sepulturas. The sculpture monuments allowed us much more information on political history than could be hoped for in sites without texts. Ironically, an excavation in the valley led us to return to the Principal Group, armed with innovative methods to tackle problems both new and old. We now have an ideal situation where research at the site core and in the valley settlements feed back and forth. Indeed, the present Acropolis research has given us leads to follow in the further investigation of the supporting urban neighborhoods and rural communities of the Copán city-state. We will pay particular attention to the inscriptions found in the valley which carry the place names cited on the four façades of the *popol na*.

But now let us turn to the explicit development of the theme of the king as warrior, in the works of the rulers who succeeded Smoke Monkey.

CHAPTER SEVEN

THE GREAT REVIVAL: THE HIEROGLYPHIC STAIRWAY

Following the death of the 13th ruler, 18 Rabbit, Copán entered a period of seeming dormancy – no new stelae were erected. Scholars had noted that after the placement of Stela D in 9.15.5.0.0 (AD 736), no further free-standing monuments were erected until Stela M, in 9.16.5.0.0 (AD 756). This was taken by some to mean that Copán went into a decline after the loss of their distinguished ruler, and was unable to marshal public labor for monuments until nearly 20 years after his death. In the previous chapter we saw how the 14th ruler, Smoke Monkey, attempted in AD 746 to reunite the valley by publicly signaling the power of the people through their representatives. In the 10 years following the dedication of the Mat House, all the artistic energy of the Copán court was focused on a very different kind of monument: the Hieroglyphic Stairway and Temple of Structure 10L-26.

The Hieroglyphic Stairway has been the subject of a great deal of research. Berthold Riese noted that the stairway is equivalent to some 20 Copán stelae in magnitude and elaboration, constituting the longest single hieroglyphic inscription of the ancient New World.[1] Maudslay first discovered it and began excavations on the west side of Structure 10L-26. In one of those great ironies of history, the glyph-block that Maudslay illustrated was the one which carries what scholars now recognize to be the Quiriguá emblem-glyph. In their expeditions of 1891 and 1895 the Peabody Museum of Harvard University was the first to excavate the stairway itself. These investigations uncovered two sets of stairs still in order, and hundreds of glyph blocks that had fallen to the bottom of the building in a jumble. A group of 15 steps had slumped down as a unit from higher up on the stairway, and covered the 15 lowest steps, which were still in place. The analysis of the glyphs contained in these two sets of still-ordered stairs, and the other miscellaneous blocks found in the uncovering of the stairway, were presented in Gordon's published report.[2] Thereafter, Morley gave a summary of the dates inscribed on the stairway in his 1920 compendium on the Copán inscriptions, and saw to it that the stairway was one of the monuments to be restored during the subsequent Carnegie Institution work at the site.

87 (Opposite) Stela M, now badly weathered and battered because of a damaging fall in antiquity. Originally one of the most graceful and refined stelae, this monument portrays the 15th ruler Smoke Shell.

88 *The Hieroglyphic Stairway, as it appeared in 1937, with only the still-ordered segments of the inscription restored.*

The restoration of the Hieroglyphic Stairway was directed by Stromsvik during the late 1930s and early 1940s. At first, only the steps that had been found in order were restored, with the bottom-most steps merely consolidated *in situ*, and the other (slumped) steps placed about two-thirds of the way up the stairway. This proved to be an unsatisfactory solution, because it meant that hundreds of blocks would be left on the surface of the site, to collect moss, deteriorate further, and be subjected to the whims of visitors to the site. Stromsvik therefore subsequently returned all the other known glyph blocks and human figure fragments back to the stairway. In doing so, the glyph blocks which made up deciphered dates in the Long Count were placed in sequence, while the rest were placed in a more or less haphazard way, to fill in the remaining spaces. Given their knowledge at the time and their concern for the

89 Reconstruction of Structure 10L-26 and Ballcourt A-III, as viewed from the summit of the final version of Structure 10L-11.

conservation and restoration – or 'repair', as they called it – this was the most responsible course of action available to them.

Another aspect of the Carnegie work on Structure 10L-26 was the excavation of the floor of the superstructure of the building, to which the stairway led. Maudslay and Gordon had believed that the entire superstructure was destroyed and had slumped down the sides of the pyramid. But in 1936, in trying to discern the original declination of the stairway, Aubrey Trik of the Carnegie staff discovered that fragments of the plaster floor inside the superstructure were still preserved. Trik then undertook the complete excavation of the temple floor. Although badly battered and slumped, meticulous restoration revealed the floor to be quite informative. Careful refitting of the floor fragments allowed Trik to define the edges of the floor, and reveal that the temple structure did in fact have an entrance on its west side, directly behind the top of the Hieroglyphic Stairway. Although the front wall of the temple had slumped, the juncture of the plaster floor with the wall was still preserved on the edges of the plaster itself, which lipped up to where the wall had originally stood. In this way, it was possible to define the sizes of the doorways, and the width of the front wall. The remnants of another wall on the east extremity of the preserved part of the floor represent either the back wall of the temple, or (more likely) the frontal step or 'bench' wall of an interior chamber to the temple.

The excavation of the temple atop Structure 10L-26 also yielded numerous sculpture fragments, fallen from the carved surfaces of the temple itself. These included a number of fragments of the very elaborate, full-figure inscription, parts of which the Peabody expeditions had also found in their earlier investigations. Based on an examination of the Peabody Museum fragments, Morley had surmised that this text originally adorned an eastern doorway of the building. Working with the newly-found fragments, and comparing them with those found by the Peabody expeditions, Morley proclaimed that this very elaborate text 'was the finest inscription ever carved in the ancient city'.[3]

The next major attempt to understand Structure 10L-26 and its corpus of monumental sculptures came during the first phase of the PAC. The Director, Claude Baudez, instructed the epigrapher Berthold Riese to do a complete epigraphic survey, concentrating on the dating of the monuments and on the dynastic history of the site. Riese realized that a number of the earlier renderings of the glyphic texts of Copán were not up to modern standards, and would need to be redrawn. Among these Riese placed the Hieroglyphic Stairway high on his list. The abundant early dates and historical material on the stairway provided information that could be compared with the texts on the standing monuments and on the buried fragments of older ones. The immense task of drawing the stairway inscription was undertaken by project artist, Barbara Fash. (Unfortunately, it was not then possible to draw the glyphs from scale photographs – the standard practice in modern hieroglyphic recording – but rather every glyph was drawn by eye.)

As Fash proceeded, Riese and Peter Mathews (another epigrapher) began to realize and assess the historical material covered in this inscription. Mathews picked out the accession date of the 12th ruler by joining together glyph blocks which had not been restored in their original places. The precise fit of the lines that formed a single glyph shared by the two now-separated blocks demonstrated beyond doubt that they were indeed originally joined. Riese used these and other data to fill in the historical sequence at the site, including the recognition of the names of several rulers on the sides of Altar Q.

The Hieroglyphic Stairway Project

In 1986, Structure 10L-26 became the focus of an intense program of new excavations, new sculpture recording in photographs and drawings, and new epigraphic studies, sponsored by a number of research institutions in the USA, and directed by the author.[4] Our goals were to address a series of inter-related research questions, while at the same time completing an exhaustive documentation of the building and its associated sculptures. The project was conceived as the first step in the process of conserving and where possible restoring both the sculptures and the structure itself. In this, we had the good fortune to enlist the help of specialists in allied fields – particularly the epigraphers – working with us on the larger Copán Mosaics Project.

Our investigations sought to resolve the question: what was the ultimate purpose and meaning of the Hieroglyphic Stairway and Temple? We set out to test two alternative hypotheses. Hypothesis 1 was that the stairway was imposed on Copán as a conquest monument by the triumphant Quiriguá dynasty in the wake of the capture and beheading of 18 Rabbit. Hypothesis 2 was that the stairway and temple represented an effort on the part of the indigenous Copán dynasty to rebuild its prestige and legitimacy, and to carry on its own dynastic and political tradition despite the loss of their revered ruler. The two hypotheses had very different implications for questions regarding the scale and motives of Late Classic warfare in the Maya lowlands. A series of expectations or 'test implications' was drawn up for each hypothesis, so that we could structure the investigations in such a way as to obtain adequate information to fully evaluate the two alternatives.

Our methods were designed to enable us to obtain accurate and detailed information on the architecture, on the sculptures which adorned it, and on associated behavioral evidence. Excavations were undertaken to uncover all four sides of the pyramidal substructure revealing architectural features, and any residues of prehistoric activity left on the structure, and the position and fall patterns of the thousands of fragments of tenoned mosaic façade sculptures that originally adorned the building at the summit of this monument. We also sought to uncover the earlier versions of the structure, presumably preserved in the core of the pyramid, in order to compare the final-phase building in all of its extravagance with its previous versions. This would give us a perspective within which to evaluate the latest version, and help us to resolve which of our hypotheses was more likely. The plotting of the sculpture enabled us to determine which side of the superstructure each fragment had fallen from. Combining this data with the refitting of adjacent pieces provided us with accurate minimum counts for the different motifs on each side of the temple. All of these were necessary steps for the longer-term goal of producing a reconstruction drawing of what the four façades of the superstructure looked like.

Each fragment was numbered, cataloged, photographed and drawn at a 1:10 scale, and stored in our laboratory alongside the other examples of its motif-class, grouped according to the side of the building it derived from. Whenever possible, the drawings were done from the earlier photographs taken by the Carnegie Institution or Peabody Museum investigators, as the older photographs showed portions of the glyphs which had eroded away in the intervening years. (All the drawings were checked by at least two other artists/epigraphers, to ensure that the published work was as accurate as possible.[5]) In addition to recording the stairway inscription, we also photographed and drew the human figures restored on the central axis of the stairway, and the elaborate, carved balustrades which frame the sides.

90 *Seated human figure from the Hieroglyphic Stairway, surrounded by rodent heads that may represent a portrait of 18 Rabbit.*

Inscriptions and imagery

Although our work on the sculptures and excavations is not finished, clear evidence has already emerged that enables us to choose between the two hypotheses. We believe that the Hieroglyphic Stairway and Temple of Structure 10L-26 were commissioned in order to record the important events in the dynastic history of Copán. What we have been able to document and reconstruct of the text cites the birth, accession to power, important rituals and other achievements, parentage statements, and death, of the most distinguished rulers of the city. At present, the inscription covers the historical events from AD 553 to 756, but there is evidence that earlier events and rulers are represented, as well. We do know that the founder of the dynasty, Yax K'uk Mo', is also cited.

The inscription takes us up to the time of commemoration of and placement at the base of the stairway of Stela M, which is a portrait of the 15th ruler, Smoke Shell. The human figures on the central axis of the stairway, and the six slightly larger-than-life-size figures which originally decorated the upper part of the temple façade, in all likelihood represent portraits of the deceased royal

91 Sculpture façade motifs from the
Hieroglyphic Temple of Structure 10L-26
and the temple annex (Structure 10L-230).
a goggle-eyed Jaguar Tlaloc mask, with fan
motifs emanating from the mouth; *b* cornice
fan motif; *c* sectioned shell; *d* stylized shell;
e rope for binding captives; *f* rectangular
feather-fringed shield; *g* ruler portrait,
complete with large shield borne in the left
hand (note rectangular bar pectoral); *h* fan
motif; *i* fleshless human long bones; *j* skull.
i and *j* are from the temple annex; the
remainder are from Structure 10L-26.

ancestors. Indeed, one of them is surrounded by images of the rodent head that
makes up the main sign of the glyph for the ruler 18 Rabbit. It may eventually
be possible to identify each of the ruler portraits, according to the symbols that
he wears or sits upon, once the documentation and study of the stairway have
been completed.

The inscription seems to emphasize the role of one Copán ruler in particular.
The commemoration date of the building is followed, not by the name of
Smoke Shell (who actually finished the monument), but by that of the
distinguished 12th ruler Smoke Imix God K. In addition, the inscription on the
bottom steps – the most-often seen and read part of the inscription –
emphasizes the life and times of Smoke Imix God K. Since Altar L of Quiriguá
shows Smoke Imix God K in a position of strength at that site, it does not seem
likely that his memory would be evoked if Quiriguá had built the Hieroglyphic
Stairway as a conquest monument. It is more probable that the 15th ruler
Smoke Shell revived the memory of the great ruler as a rallying cry to unite all
his people.

The inscription, insofar as we can tell, does not record the name, accession, or other important date of a single ruler from Quiriguá. The death of 18 Rabbit is cited, but in the context of bemoaning his loss in battle. Indeed, given the apparent hegemony of Smoke Imix God K over Quiriguá, we are left wondering whether the possible Quiriguá emblem-glyph cited in one of the loose blocks of the stairway might in fact have been a title born in the name-phrase of one of the Copán rulers. This practice has been documented for the 11th ruler, Butz' Chan, and for the 13th ruler, 18 Rabbit, both of whom cite the main sign of the Los Higos (in the La Venta Valley) title or emblem-glyph in their title strings.

Thus, it appears all but certain that the Hieroglyphic Stairway was an indigenous Copán dynasty monument, built to relegitimize their ruling order in the face of the humiliating loss of 18 Rabbit. Indeed, the building and its elaborate decorations have the feeling of a revivalist movement, erected to galvanize support behind the royal line and its governing system. The portraits of the rulers serve to identify the distinguished historical personages whose accomplishments are duly noted in the lengthy hieroglyphic text. The portraits also stress the roles of the royal ancestors as great warriors, for virtually all of them carry shields in their left hands. The figure still *in situ* at the base of the stairway (which, some of our staff conjecture, may represent Smoke Imix God K) still had his right forearm and hand, held out perpendicular to the body, with the thumb and fingers held as if grasping a thin, vertical object. Given the canons of Late Classic Maya art, it seems likely that he grasped a lance, one such as those held by the warriors on the murals of Bonampak, or on any number of other Maya images of the king as warrior. Another of the portrait figures was surrounded by sculptures of ropes, such as those used for binding war captives before sacrifice. The central headdress element of another figure was the so-called 'year-sign', proven by Proskouriakoff to be associated with Maya warriors.[6]

Thus the main theme of the temple decoration is that of royal ancestor worship, embedded in the context of war and sacrifice. Complementing the portraits of the royal ancestors as warriors were six large masks of the goggle-eyed deity known as 'Tlaloc' in Central Mexico. Esther Pasztory has divided images of Tlaloc into two types: the 'Jaguar-Tlaloc', associated with scenes of warfare and sacrifice; and the 'Crocodile-Tlaloc', found in imagery devoted to themes of fertility and natural abundance.[7] In the Maya area, only the Jaguar Tlaloc is represented, and Schele believes it to be the patron of warriors who procure human captives for sacrifice. The Tlaloc masks on Structure 10L-26 were prominently placed on the four corners of the temple, and over the doorways of the structure on its front and back sides. Rounding out the imagery were shells (symbolic of the watery Underworld), rectangular feathered shields, and what have been interpreted by some as blood scrolls. The whole complex of symbols was designed to show that all the Copán rulers were consummate warriors and procurers of victims for sacrifice.

92 *Eccentric flints from the Hieroglyphic Stairway cache.*

The archaeological evidence

The archaeological excavations produced material remains of activities which tend to support the above interpretations. In his 1987 excavations underneath the altar that forms the base of the Hieroglyphic Stairway, David Stuart uncovered the offertory cache placed there when the stairway was commemorated. Comprising one of the finest ceremonial offerings ever uncovered at the ancient city, this cache contained some very important clues about the building and its meaning to the king who commemorated it. The cache was placed under a stone cap directly underneath the altar, and included: a lidded ceramic censer containing two jadeite pieces, a lanceolate flint knife, a shell, some ash and carbon, and some sting-ray and sea urchin spines. Carefully placed next to the ceramic vessel were three elaborately chipped eccentric flints. The objects selected for burial all had a strong symbolic value, and can be related to the images and messages of the overall monument.

The three eccentric flints are among the finest examples of this exquisite art form yet uncovered, each displaying seven Classic Maya heads depicted in profile. The flints are lanceolate in form, and from the size of their tangs it is obvious that they were hafted to some sort of shaft, in all probability a long

93 *Spiny oyster shell* (Spondylus sp.)*, and sting-ray and sea urchin spines from the Hieroglyphic Stairway cache. Spiny oyster shells such as these are frequently found in offerings associated with the ancestors, presumably being symbolic of the watery Underworld.*

lance. The amount of skill required to produce objects of this sort is beyond the capability of any present-day flint-knapper, and must have been exceptional, even in Classic Maya cities such as Copán. Thus, the individual who bore such a lance was distinguished indeed. (These were symbolic weapons worthy of divine warriors, and I would argue that some of the stairway portrait figures carried lances topped with eccentrics such as these.)

The two jade pieces placed inside the stone censer were heirlooms, the style of which indicates that they were carved in the 4th or 5th century AD. The smaller piece is a charming and marvelously naturalistic statuette of a human figure, with a simple cloth headband and breechclout. This presumably represents a portrait figure, though of whom in particular we can only speculate. The larger piece is a bar pectoral pendant, drilled transversely so that it could be strung and worn on the chest. Pectorals of the same type and size were carved on the chests of all the ruler portraits from the temple. It seems likely that this particular jade pendant was used by a number of the ancestors portrayed on the monument, since it was about 300 years old by the time Smoke Shell placed it in the cache. The same may or may not be true of the other jade.

The censer, sting-ray and sea-urchin spines, and shell can also be related to the symbolism of the structure itself. The sting-ray spines, and probably also the sea-urchin spines, would have been used in auto-sacrificial bloodletting rituals. Such rituals probably occurred at or close to the time the cache objects were buried. Such bloodletting was closely tied in with both the worship of the royal ancestors and with Jaguar Tlaloc war and sacrifice symbolism. Stuart and Schele have also noted that the base of the stairway itself represents an elaborate inverted Tlaloc head. The figures and entire stairway inscription are being belched forth out of the open mouth of this beast, whose lower jaw was at the top of the steps. According to Stuart the figures were being made to appear in a vision produced by the auto-sacrifice of the living ruler.[8] The cache was placed inside the head of the Jaguar Tlaloc, precisely where its brain would be located. The auto-sacrificial rite was thus the engine behind the production of the vision.

Lastly, the spiny oyster shell in the cache played its part in the symbolism of the inauguration ceremony. The ash and carbon in the censer were the residue of burning incense and possibly bark-paper spattered with Smoke Shell's blood.[9] The shell held red pigment, and was also engulfed in smoke during the ritual. The Mayanist Eric Thompson always insisted that the Maya loved a good pun, and this 'smoking shell' of Smoke Shell appears to be one of them.

Further confirmation of the importance of sacrifice is found in the iconography and material remains of Structure 10L-230, which had been added on the south side of Structure 10L-26. Structure 10L-230 was decorated with sculptures of numerous human skulls, over 100 fleshless human long bones, and the glyph sign *na* (house). On the floor of the central chamber of this 'house of human bones and skulls' was found a small censer and a broken eccentric flint knife. Although no remains of sacrificed bodies were found, these objects indicate that ritual did take place in the structure, which must have been linked with grisly sacrificial rituals, as a place of sacrifice, storage, dismemberment, embalming, or other manipulations of human remains.

A final interesting aspect of Structure 10L-26 is the marked contrast between its final version and that of its antecedents. Significant parts of the earlier structures were preserved within the fill of the final pyramid platform. Although the very earliest building had a hieroglyphic step – placed by Cu Ix in front of Yax K'uk Mo's 9 Baktun Period Ending stela – none of the buildings had hieroglyphic texts on their exteriors as the final version did. Nor, so far as we know, did the earlier versions have ruler portraits. What substructure decoration we have comprises plaster sculptures of non-human entities: G1 masks, the Principal Bird deity, and a giant crocodile spanning the east side of Papagayo Structure. Thus, the substructure decoration of these earlier buildings was cosmological in theme, in marked contrast to the final structure.

This dramatic change in imagery indicates that the loss of Copán's 13th god-king at the hands of a former vassal literally shook the ideological system to its foundations, provoking a radical departure from previous patterns. And yet, when one looks at the message given in the new medium, it is still a very traditional one: that the strength of the city lay in the supernatural and in the secular strength of its warrior rulers. This was truly a revivalist monument, bringing the city back to its roots by renewing the images, history, and glory of its great ancestral kings.

But the question of the veracity of our interpretations of such evidence is one which continues to sow dissension among modern students of the ancient Maya. Many scholars lament the renewed interest in written records and state art, insisting that they are political propaganda and should not be given undue credence as fact. Although the Hieroglyphic Stairway and Temple of Structure 10L-26 was indeed an impressive revivalist temple, it also brings to mind Shakespeare's immortal line about the lady that doth protest too much. If Copán's kings were all great warriors, and the dynastic history so distinguished and grand, why belabor the point in such monumental fashion?

The fact is, the fill used to support the stairway and façades of this building was the weakest we have found in the Principal Group: instead of mud mortar, the stones are set in loose, dry earth, poorly or incompletely consolidated. It is a telling irony that the only major stairway at the site which collapsed was the one which the last rulers had most hoped would be everlasting. For despite its grandeur, the archaeological data from Structure 10L-26 suggest that the *ah holpop* and the people they represented were less than wildly enthusiastic in their support of Smoke Shell and his unique monument.

Perspectives from Copán and Quiriguá on Classic Maya warfare

And what of Quiriguá, the cause of all the fuss and the reason for this grandiose gesture in the first place? Since Morley's time, scholars had maintained that Quiriguá was a colony of Copán, on the basis that the core areas of each were virtually identical in layout. Quiriguá, built along the banks of the river that gave it life, also boasts a Great Plaza with elaborate stelae and altars, and has a ballcourt at the foot of its Acropolis. But let us examine the similarities of the two sites within the context of the new historical information provided by the epigraphic breakthroughs of the past three decades. Rather than being a colony of Copán, somehow obliged by its mentor to *emulate* its example, it now appears more likely that the imitation was a deliberate ploy by Quiriguá's ruler Cauac Sky to outdo his former masters from Copán.

The similarities start at the very entrances to the centers. At Copán, the eastern entrance to the site core coincides with the end of the *sacbe* (paved road) leading from the densely settled residential area of Las Sepulturas. At this crossroads stands Stela J, on whose western side is carved a mat pattern, with hieroglyphs intertwined on two separate strips, just as if they had been woven into a mat. This symbol of royal power forms an appropriate icon for an inscription placed at the entrance to the city of the newly-inaugurated ruler. The inscription records the first major Period Ending after the accession of 18 Rabbit, and constitutes his first monument in the Principal Group. At Quiriguá, Stela H was placed at the eastern entrance to the site core, where the canoe port on the Motagua River is believed to have stood.[10] Carved on Stela H's eastern side is a mat weave, simpler than that on Copán's Stela J, but an obvious imitation. The text records Cauac Sky's first major Period Ending after his accession, again in direct imitation of the Copán example.

The famous capture and decapitation of 18 Rabbit occurred some 12 years later, and Cauac Sky seems to have reaped a political windfall from the event. He commemorated a number of stelae in his Great Plaza, and sought to outdo his deceased rival by erecting some of the tallest examples ever carved. Stela E, for example, stands 11 m high. On the base of one of these stelae, Cauac Sky notes that he acceded to power 'in the land of 18 Rabbit', suggesting that Quiriguá had indeed been a vassal of Copán before Cauac Sky so dramatically declared his political independence.[11] He makes a point of citing the decapitation date five times on his Great Plaza monuments, and on one occasion even goes so far as to claim the Copán emblem-glyph in one of his own title strings.

Around the Great Plaza Cauac Sky also seems to have embarked on an ambitious building spree, and in retrospect it appears that he was trying to build another Copán, but on a larger, more impressive scale: with a considerably bigger Great Plaza, taller stelae, larger zoomorphic altars, marble temples, and other monuments. There is no evidence, however, that Quiriguá received any massive influx of goods or people from Copán at this time. Copador polychrome pottery, the main export from the Copán Valley from the time of 18 Rabbit or earlier, is extremely rare at Quiriguá, even at the site core.[12] Likewise, although the population of Quiriguá did expand considerably at this time, it never attained more than a quarter that of Copán, and the settlement forms remained distinctively local.[13] There is a possibility that some of the lands formerly belonging to Copán were usurped by Cauac Sky in the wake of his victory, but the presence of Copador pottery even as far north as sites on the Morjá River – closer to Quiriguá than to Copán, and part of the Motagua drainage system – indicates that resource areas between the two still preferred to interact with Copán.

This evidence from Copán and Quiriguá argues strongly that material incentives, rather than just some form of ritual jousting between rival rulers, were the cause of Late Classic Maya warfare. By capturing and beheading the Copán king who had been his master, Cauac Sky obtained his political independence. His prowess as a warrior and leader gave him success just as the forays of Butz' Chan into the La Venta Valley, and of the 3rd and 4th Copán rulers to Quiriguá may have been a major part of their success. It would appear that for the Classic Maya, warfare was a highly charged mechanism for political control, as it has been for numerous other societies throughout history. When one looks at Copán's most ostentatious response to humiliating defeat, what does one find but portraits of the earlier, ancestral rulers as successful warriors!

94 Smoke Shell, as portrayed on his last monument, Stela N.

CHAPTER EIGHT

LIFE UNDER YAX PAC

The final ruler in the dynasty of K'inich Yax K'uk Mo' was Yax Pac, the 16th ruler, whose Maya name means 'First Dawn'.[1] On Copán Stela 8, we find glyphs which state that he was the son of a woman from Palenque, near the Usumacinta River in modern Chiapas. As another means of status reinforcement, his predecessor and father, Smoke Shell, had married a woman from the Palenque royal house, in order to bring added prestige to his offspring. He was to be the last, and in many ways most celebrated, dynast of Copán.

The written record for Yax Pac is the most abundant in the city's history, a reflection on both the productivity of his scribes and artists, and the fact that his monuments were not covered over or buried by any successors. There are numerous texts and politically-charged sculptured façades from both the Principal Group and from élite-level residential compounds in the valley. The valley inscriptions provide insights into the methods of political patronage used by Yax Pac, to hold his kingdom together during troubled times. Similarly, other texts illuminate the relationship of Copán to some of the large residential compounds in the rural hinterland, particularly to Los Higos and Río Amarillo. Beyond the hieroglyphic texts, study of the valley settlements also provides abundant information about the supporting population that the inscriptions and imagery do not touch upon. Indeed, the vistas of ancient Copanec society and demography provided by archaeology serve as a baseline from which to evaluate the cultural and political changes that took place during Yax Pac's reign.

Settlement patterns during the reign of Yax Pac

The study of settlement patterns in the Copán Valley provides an enormous amount of data on the nature of social, political, economic, and religious organization during the reign of Yax Pac. The mapping of ancient settlements and other cultural features, and the selective excavation of representative samples of the population, have allowed archaeologists to obtain a much better understanding of Copán as a city, rather than simply as a ceremonial center.

Within the Copán pocket, an area of 24 sq. km was intensely surveyed, and all visible cultural features carefully mapped. The remains of a total of 3414 individual mounds were located and mapped, in addition to such features as ancient terraces, roads, outlying stelae and their respective platforms.[2] Using a

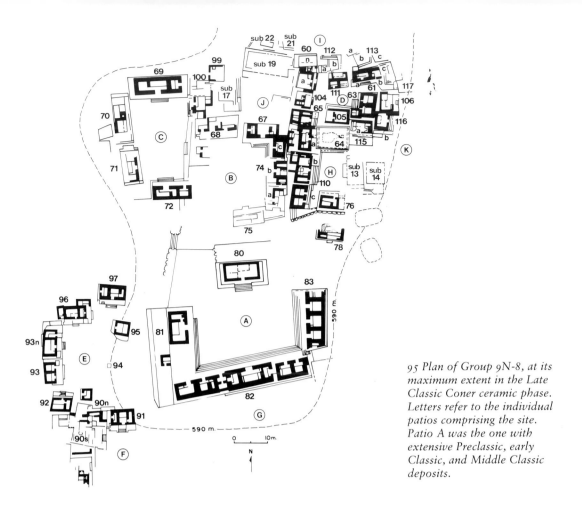

95 Plan of Group 9N-8, at its maximum extent in the Late Classic Coner ceramic phase. Letters refer to the individual patios comprising the site. Patio A was the one with extensive Preclassic, early Classic, and Middle Classic deposits.

variety of different procedures, a number of population estimates have been made for the ancient population of the Copán pocket. After some marked fluctuations during the early years of the valley surveys, most of the estimates now are in the range of 20,000 inhabitants for the peak population around AD 800.

Gordon Willey's and Richard Leventhal's early work devised a typology of the valley sites which distinguishes large, élite residential groups (Type 3 and 4 sites) and smaller, less ostentatious residential groups (Type 1 and 2 sites), occupied by the majority of the population. Some Type 3 sites boast vaulted structures, occasionally embellished with sculptures, but it is Type 4 sites that have the greatest number of buildings, the most elaborate architecture, and – at least in the densely-populated areas to either side of the Principal Group – the longest history of occupation. Group 9N-8 of the Sepulturas ward east of the Principal Group is the paramount example of a Type 4 group, with occupations stretching back to the Early Preclassic period and culminating in an extensive Late Classic residential group, with a profusely decorated palace structure serving as the residence and temple of the patriarch of the lineage which occupied the site (see Chapters Four to Six).

In general, one may divide the settlement pattern of the late 8th-century Copán pocket into two basic components: the densely-occupied urban core (within a 1-km radius from the center of the Principal Group to lands north of the river[3]) containing the majority of the élite residential compounds in the valley; and a non-urban or rural sector, exhibiting progressively less dense occupations as one proceeds away from the center. This conforms well with Bishop Landa's descriptions of 16th-century Yucatec towns, and with the pattern observed in the settlement and distribution of the élite-level vaulted structures at the Classic-period site of Dzibilchaltun, in northern Yucatán.[4]

Within these urban and rural areas, there was considerable variation in settlement density. For example, the foothills directly north of the Principal Group do not exhibit as many visible structures as do the alluvial bottomlands to the east and west of the site core. For this reason, Sanders considers this section to be part of a 'sub-urban fringe'.[5] However, post-abandonment soil erosion has caused many of the ancient settlements in this area to be covered by as much as 2 m of overburden, and the modern landscape may not accurately reflect the density of the original occupation. The presence of a *sacbe* and

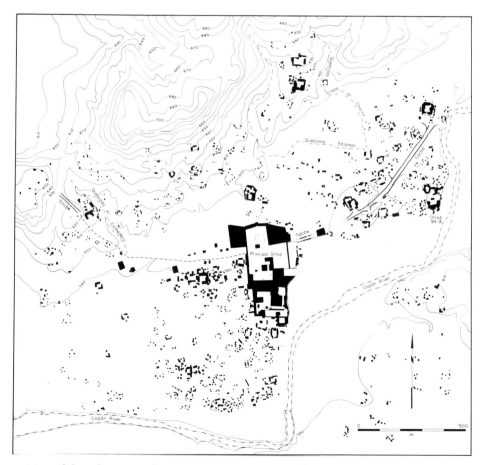

96 *Map of the urban core of ancient Copán, comprising all the structures within a 1-km radius of the center of the Principal Group, Ballcourt A-III.*

several Type 3 and 4 sites also argues for urban status and the author considers this area part of the urban nucleus. We also know that the large alluvial fan presently occupied by the village of Copán Ruinas, which on the above criteria would be considered rural, was in fact densely inhabited in ancient times, including pyramidal structures and numerous inscribed, sculptured monuments.[6] Indeed, the older villagers say that at the turn of the century, the determining factor for deciding where to build one's house was to try to find a spot with no mounds in which to set to work! The rapid growth of the village has eliminated all Late Classic architecture from the modern landscape, however, and Morley's and Longyear's maps only record areas with monumental architecture. In the rural parts of the Copán pocket, there are several large sites and some densely occupied areas, and at least two sites with elaborate sculptures (Rastrojón and Ostumán).

Internal organization of the ancient city

There are two paved roads leading into the Principal Group, one on the east leading in from a Type 4 site which defines the eastern limit of the Sepulturas ward; and the other on the west, originating at a Type 4 site which marks the northwestern limit of the Comedero ward. Other than these roadways, however, there is nothing to indicate any kind of centralized planning in the layout and construction of the residential wards and outlying shrines and temples in the valley. There is certainly nothing approximating a grid-plan for the city of Copán: individual sites and wards all exhibit a haphazard arrangement.

In attempting to produce order out of such seeming chaos, to explain the settlement patterns and system of the Late Classic Copán Valley, I have looked to the ethnographic evidence for an analogy. The best source seemed to be the Chortí people, now concentrated in eastern Guatemala and descendants of the Classic-period southeastern Maya. The Chortí occupy the same type of environmental setting as the one inhabited by the ancient Copanecs, and show cultural continuity with their ancestors in both the material and spiritual realms, documented by Charles Wisdom in his monograph *The Chortí Indians of Guatemala*.[7] This area is geographically contiguous with the Copán pocket, and includes the lower reaches of the Copán Valley before reaching the Motagua River. It is physiographically similar, with intermittent and permanent stream systems criss-crossing mountains and rolling terrain.

Among the Chortí, Wisdom found a series of towns and sub-communities occupying the areas between the towns. These sub-communities are called *sian otot* (many houses), and an area within them *ta sian otot* (many houses place). Each *sian otot* is made up of a number of fairly self-sufficient families, each with its group of houses and surrounding maize fields, gardens, and orchards. Each *sian otot* occupies a single geographic area, and considers all the land and resources within that area their own. Marriage is generally between members

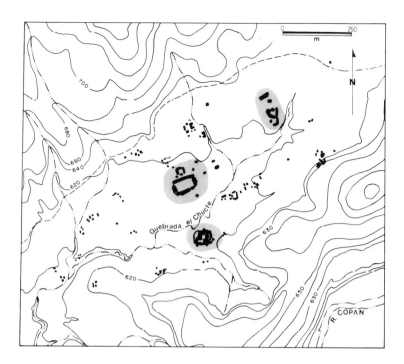

97 Plan of the sian otot *(sub-community) of Ostuman. Shading indicates the paired Type 3 and 4 sites.*

of the same sub-community, so that most of the people are interrelated by marriage or by blood, or both. Each of the sub-communities contains about 25 families, made up of 60 to 80 households, though Wisdom notes that some are three or four times larger than others. Within the *sian otot*, families often cluster together in small groups, leaving large spaces nearly unoccupied. There is no formal site planning or layout within the sub-community, and nothing that could be called streets or a central plaza. The trails that connect the different households and families simply wind through them on their way to other sub-communities, and the families are located as close to these trails as possible.

Specific socio-geographic units, probably similar to these Chortí sub-communities, can be recognized in the Late Classic settlements in the Copán pocket. The first such unit to be identified was the Sepulturas ward defined by Willey and Leventhal, consisting of a number of residential groups laid out along either side of the eastern *sacbe* of the city. Another is the El Bosque ward, just west of the Principal Group, and a third one adjacent to the site core is the swath of foothills directly north of it. The alluvial fan occupied by the modern village constitutes a fourth very large sub-community. The remaining 16 that have been defined in the Copán pocket are closer to the size described by Wisdom for the modern Chortí. These 20 sub-communities all occupy a discrete physiographic segment of the Copán pocket, such as the *quebrada* (ravine) sections described by Leventhal,[8] and the intra-montane pockets of Ostumán and Petapilla defined by B.L. Turner and the ecological team of the Harvard and PAC I projects.[9]

Of considerable interest is that many of the proposed sub-communities are centered around a pair of large sites, generally of Type 3 and 4, although smaller sub-communities all have Type 2 sites at their core. Returning to the case of the Chortí, Wisdom records that it is usual for two families to intermarry, the children of one marrying the children of the same generation in the other (though there are exceptions). Wisdom notes that this kinship system fits the preferred marriage system based on sibling and cousin exchange. A similar system seems to be implied in the ancient Copán pocket by the archaeological evidence, namely marriage bonds between pairs of extended families, Type 3 and 4 sites representing the residences of the oldest segments of the family, and Type 1 and 2 sites the smaller segments which broke off and were scattered through the sub-community. As Leventhal noted, the large sites presumably contained the most important lineage shrines for their respective sections of the valley, adding to their importance not only within their own sub-community, but for the city of Copán as a whole.[10]

This model of 'organic growth' for the ancient sub-communities is supported by the fact that the larger sites generally tend to have longer occupation sequences than the smaller ones. Similarly, the organic growth of the valley population during the Classic period seems to have begun in the bottomlands north of the river, in the east part of the pocket, expanding to the foothills area north of the Principal Group (including the area where the modern village stands), and from there to the *quebrada* sections and intra-montane pockets farther afield. Finally, the pockets of fertile alluvial soils formed by the tributaries of the Copán River were occupied as the population expanded and the arable land in the Copán pocket was swallowed up during the growth of the city.

Economic specialization in the urban wards

Many sociologists and anthropologists follow Louis Wirth in defining cities as having three distinctive features: large population size; dense population nucleation; and high internal heterogeneity.[11] While Copán under Yax Pac qualifies on the first two points, there is still much discussion of the degree of internal heterogeneity, especially in terms of economic specialization within and between the different sub-communities. The rural sub-communities of the Copán pocket had enough arable land in their immediate vicinities to be agriculturally self-sufficient. The same may not have been true for the three communities that formed the urban nucleus of Copán, where more land was relegated to construction than to farming. Not surprisingly, it is in the urban core that we have archaeological evidence for different kinds of specialists: scribes, shell workers, ballplayers, etc. We have not yet found any kilns or other direct evidence for ceramic production areas, yet this is a field where most scholars agree that Copán was very productive.

With the emergence of Copador polychrome pottery as a prized commodity

– found in households of all socio-economic strata in the Copán Valley – Copán is believed to have become a regional center for its production and redistribution. Neutron activation analysis by Ronald Bishop suggests that the clay sources used in the production of Copador polychrome were to be found somewhere in the Copán Valley. Following this line of reasoning, Copán is thought to have engaged in, if not dominated, exchange systems with numerous localities in the southeast periphery of the Maya area, where Copador pottery is found in greatest frequency and variety. Arthur Demarest has pursued this further, suggesting that through the acquisition and redistribution of Copador pottery, and pilgrimages to Copán, other nascent or established élites in western El Salvador, and western and central Honduras, were able to reinforce their own status through contacts with and emulation of the royal house of Copán.[12] This idea has much support at Copán, where evidence of contacts with the non-Maya speakers to the east and south is abundant in the archaeological record.

Large quantities of central Honduran Ulua (or Ulua-Yojoa) polychrome potsherds and whole vessels have been found in excavations throughout the Copán pocket. They are not restricted to élite contexts, or even to burial contexts, but show up in the middens of even the most humble house-mounds on the outskirts of the pocket.[13] Thus, exchange with areas to the south and east resulted in the importation of great quantities of polychrome pottery, and possibly of other commodities as well. During Sanders' PAC II work, Andrea Gerstle and David Webster excavated a courtyard in Group 9N-8 which may have housed immigrants from central Honduras. This Patio D appears to provide compelling evidence for a patron–client socio-economic system in 8th-century Copán. Higher concentrations of Ulua polychrome ceramics were found here than anywhere else in the valley, and a distinctively non-Maya (Lower Central American) tripod grinding stone – unlike any other found in Copán – was also recovered.

Some distinctive architectural forms and burial patterns also point to non-Maya origins for Patio D's residents. The family or other corporate group in question was apparently attached to the larger, indigenous élite lineage which owned and resided in the elevated patios of Group 9N-8. They seem to have been kept at something of a social distance, since there was no direct access from Patio D to the central part of the site. The conclusion has been drawn that the Patio D residents were clients who were dependent upon and lived with the long-established élite land-holding lineage immortalized in the House of the Bacabs.

Other evidence of economic specialization in Group 9N-8 comes in the form of a shell workshop discovered by Randolph Widmer in Structure 9N-110 B, of Patio H, adjacent to Patio D. On the floor of this structure was the débitage of shells that were made into ornaments, including one broken pendant remarkably similar to those depicted on the pillars supporting the nearby hieroglyphic bench in the House of the Bacabs. Besides the shell there were countless minute fragments of the obsidian tools that had been used in the manufacture of the shell ornaments. Widmer believes the production was strictly for local consumption, and does not constitute evidence of full-time craft specialization. The same conclusion was arrived at by Jack Mallory regarding extensive obsidian débitage found at a rural site he excavated in the hills of Rastrojón, northeast of the Principal Group. Whatever the activity carried out there, Mallory concluded that it was temporary, perhaps even seasonal, in nature, and not indicative of any full-time occupational specialization.

The debate continues on the subject of the degree of economic specialization at Classic Maya cities – rightly so, considering the dearth of thoroughly excavated household remains where evidence of specialization might be found. And the problem is compounded because many of the commodities known to have been most prized in Mesoamerica – textiles, for example – were perishable, and unlikely to leave any direct evidence in the archaeological record of a tropical zone. What we can say at this point is that there *were* specialists at Group 9N-8, including a shell-worker, the scribes occupying the House of the Bacabs through at least two generations, and the non-native clients of Patio D with access to imported polychrome pottery and other artifacts. How much time they dedicated to their respective specialties is a question that may never be resolved, but may profitably be studied through the excavation of similar contexts at Copán and other Maya sites.

Given the important role of merchants in Aztec society, and the evidence for long-distance exchange networks in Mesoamerica beginning in the Early Preclassic, it seems reasonable to expect that merchants might have been prominent members of Classic-period Copán society, as well. It bears noting that although polychromes from other production areas in the southeastern periphery enjoy a wide distribution in the Copán Valley, polychromes imported from other lowland Maya centers are exceedingly rare. Those which have been found derive either from the Principal Group or from élite-class residential groups in the urban core of Copán. Demarest's model of status reinforcement may also apply to the Copán élites, who through acquisition of lowland Classic Maya objects sought to reify their exalted positions.

Political patronage in the Copán Valley

The hieroglyphic evidence for interaction between the important lineage heads in the valley and the last ruler of Copán reveal the existence and potential importance of royal patronage. I would also suggest that they provide evidence for a visible weakening of centralized rule just before its demise. Descriptions of the public acts of the ruler at the hearths of his most important subjects were literally carved in stone, leaving a clear imprint in the archaeological record.

The first evidence of interaction between an élite family and the royal line was the hieroglyphic bench discovered at Structure CV-43 A in 1977.[14] Placed

98 The inscribed hieroglyphic bench from Structure 9N-82 C 1st, which cites the genealogy of the scribe (Mac Chaanal) who lived there, and his standing as a courtier of the 16th ruler, Yax Pac. This 16-glyph text represents one of the finest extant examples of the art of Maya hieroglyphic writing.

at the southern end of a large Type 3 site in Sepulturas ward, Structure CV-43 A and its full-figure hieroglyphic inscription serve as testimony to the concern of the last two Copán rulers for the welfare of their subjects residing at this site. Peter Mathews has deciphered the second date of the text, its accompanying verb, and the protagonist of that event: 9.17.10.0.0 12 Ahau 8 Pax (AD 782), 'scattering', and Yax Pac, respectively. Subsequent work on this text by Floyd Lounsbury, Schele, Stuart, and Stephen Houston has resulted in the additional reading of the first date as 9.16.10.13.10 11 Oc 13 Pax (AD 761), and the recognition that the ruler Smoke Shell (ruling at that date) designated the CV-43 lineage head as his *ah k'ul na*, or courtier. This same title, Houston and Stuart note, was also given to the Group 9N-8 scribe by Yax Pac, as duly noted on Structure 9N-82's hieroglyphic bench. An exotic, rectangular clay incense burner had been placed in the fill of CV-43 Structure A, which Yax Pac subsequently came to dedicate and christen with a 'scattering' ritual. In this fashion the 16th dynast demonstrated the royal house's concern for these prominent citizens by performing a Period Ending ceremony within the confines of their own compound, sanctifying the monument by recording his own actions there, as well as acknowledging the importance accorded the local lineage held by his predecessor, Smoke Shell.

Another, even more elaborate hieroglyphic bench was uncovered in 1981 in the House of the Bacabs (Structure 9N-82) also in Sepulturas ward. As noted above, the head of this particular lineage is believed to have had sufficient land holdings or other sources of wealth to attract clients to his residential group from outside his immediate family, and even from outside the Copán pocket. Of the people within his inner circle, at least two were of sufficient status to merit having sculptured adornment on their own buildings. The largest structures of Patios B and C were both embellished with sculpture, including a hieroglyphic text on the exterior façade of Patio C Structure 9N-69. But Structure 9N-82 was clearly the abode of the lineage head, and its sculpture gives us an invaluable record of his genealogy and interaction with Yax Pac.

The inscription on Structure 9N-82 contains 16 full-figure hieroglyphs, and is sustained by six pillars carved with the images of 'Atlantean' figures. The text begins with a Calendar Round date falling within the reign of Yax Pac, followed by the verb and the name of the protagonist. The verb contains the compound *yotot*, long recognized in the codices as meaning 'in the house (or temple)'. The event, then, takes place within the structure, and is assumed to relate to the dedication of the building itself. The name of the protagonist – Mac Chaanal – is one that does not appear in any of the texts from the Principal Group. Its only other known occurrence is on the inscription from Altar W', which was originally placed in front of this structure. The glyph following the protagonist's name is a 'child of mother' expression, with the mother being identified as 'Lady Na Kin Ahau'. Following the name of the mother is that of the father, a reference to the fact that the son is a 'successor' of the father (as a scribe; see Chapter Six) and a final clause at the end of the text interpreted by Houston and Stuart to mean that Mac Chaanal was a courtier of Yax Pac, who is named as the reigning king. The façade and bench iconography, the burial of the father and the statue of his scribal patron inside the earlier version of the building, and the bench inscription itself all indicate that Copán's élite were involved in ancestor and lineage patron worship, and able to commission and dedicate finely-carved sculptured monuments in their own honor.

An even more striking case of the importance of élites residing outside the Principal Group comes from the site now occupied by the modern village, Morley's 'Group 9'. Altars T and U were both found in this area, and it has long been known that Yax Pac's *i katun* anniversary (9.17.12.5.17) is recorded on Altar T. But it is only recently that Stuart and Schele have shown that an entirely different person is the focus of both these altars. Named with a crossed-bands sign, sky, and a skull glyph – read as Yahau Chan Ah Bac by the epigraphers – this individual is named in association with the Period Ending 9.18.5.0.0 (AD 795), and an inaugural or 'seating' event that took place within five years of that date. The office into which he accedes is not that of the high king, and his parentage statement indicates that he is the son of Yax Pac's mother (the woman from Palenque), but possibly sired by a different father (presumably after the death of Smoke Shell in AD 763). The inscriptions suggest that he is an *ahau* (lord) who is eligible to carry the Copán emblem-glyph, but who holds office under the authority of Yax Pac.

The largest structure in the Cementerio area south of the Acropolis is 10L-32, a vaulted masonry building adorned with an elaborate sculptured façade,

99 *An inscribed stone found inside Structure 10L-22A. The inscription cites Yax Pac, and his two brothers Yahau Chan Ah Bac and Yax Kamlay. All three carry the Copán emblem-glyph in their titles, indicating at least a degree of power-sharing by the 16th ruler with his brothers. The presence of this stone inside the Mat House highlights the importance of these two individuals in Yax Pac's political scheme.*

next to which were found two hieroglyphic texts. One of these, known as Altar F', cites a 'Chac' in association with the presentation of an offering made on 9.17.4.1.11 2 Chuen 4 Pop (AD 774); and his 'accession' to a non-royal office 'in the company of Yax Pac'.[15] Another altar discovered nearby by E. Wyllys Andrews of Tulane University's Middle American Research Institute also cites 'Chac' in the context of a bloodletting event performed by Yax Pac. At this point, some epigraphers believe Chac was a sibling of Yax Pac, while others believe that Structure 10L-32 and Andrews' new altar are dedicated to Chac, the Maya Rain God. If Chac turns out to be Yax Pac's brother, the proximity of this building to the Acropolis, and the inscriptions would constitute very public manifestations of his importance and power during the reign of the 16th ruler. Continuing investigations may shed further light on the role and activities of this individual.

Apparently by AD 782, Yax Pac was preoccupied with confirming his authority throughout the valley by allowing his subordinates to erect inscribed monuments which emphasize their association with him. Furthermore, the depiction of *Pauahtuns* (Maya mythological earth-bearers of the four cardinal points), and of two-headed monsters, on benches and temple façades bespeaks an effort to lock each of the noble lines into the larger cosmological, as well as

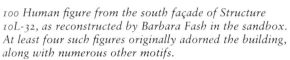

100 *Human figure from the south façade of Structure 10L-32, as reconstructed by Barbara Fash in the sandbox. At least four such figures originally adorned the building, along with numerous other motifs.*

101 *(Right) Pauahtun figures from Structure 9N-82 C 1st. The net-bag headdress (*pauah*) and stone sign (*tun*) on the shoulder of the left-hand figure identify this individual as one of the deities charged with upholding the surface of the earth (note the upraised hand, supporting the belly-scales of the saurian deity that represents the surface of the earth).*

102 *(Below) Structure 10L-32, as restored by the Copán Acropolis Archaeological Project in 1990. The upper portion of this building originally carried a great deal of elaborate sculpture.*

the local secular, order. The metaphor of the *Bacabs* (literally 'stood-up') and *Pauahtuns* seems to be that Yax Pac saw the landed nobles of the valley as pillars of the community, who were allowed the trappings of supernatural authority to ensure their continuing loyalty – and tribute – to the Copán throne.

There are important implications for the political organization of Copán to be derived from this archaeological and epigraphic data. It is noteworthy that neither the Group 9N-8 nor the CV-43 inscribed bench texts use the titles *holpop* (head of the *popol na*, the Mat House or 'Community House'), *bacab*, or *sahal* (war chief). Likewise, neither text refers to any of the non-calendric place-, lineage- or supernatural patron-glyphs that appear on the façades of Structure 22A. This would appear to indicate that neither of these residential compounds was the seat of a representative in the Mat House, which carries the further implication that the title *ah k'ul na* was for individuals one level below the representatives in the Mat House. Thus, the political hierarchy of 8th-century Copán would seem to have been structured in four tiers. At the top was the ruler and his immediate family, from which the heir to the throne was usually selected, brothers of the king being designated as governors of particular areas. Immediately below were the *holpopob* or *batabob*, who served as representatives in the deliberations at the Mat House. Next came the *ah k'ul na* or 'courtiers' – landed élites considered to be members of the court but who did not play a prominent role in the Mat House. And at the bottom were the common people, who were not given the benefit of inscribed monuments in their own honor. These four levels accord well with the definition of state-level organization followed by most anthropologists.

Relations with the hinterland

Outside the Copán pocket, the sites of Los Higos and Río Amarillo also commemorated sculptured monuments at this time. Morley's view of these sites was that they constituted outposts or satellites of Copán, and were dependent upon it.[16] More recently, Gary Pahl has concluded that the recording of some possibly non-Copán emblem-glyphs on the monuments of both sites indicates attempts on the part of those élites to establish fiefdoms of their own, independent from Copán. Both sites were situated on the edges of large tracts of fertile alluvial bottomland and, provided they could attract a large labor force, they could well have begun to prosper on their own. Still, one is struck by the strong similarity in sculpture style among the Los Higos stela, the tenoned mosaic façade sculptures found at Río Amarillo, and the examples from Copán upon which they were modeled. Also, Río Amarillo Altar 1 cites the Copán emblem-glyph, and the Pennsylvania State team's survey work has shown that there was never a large resident population in the Río Amarillo Valley. Finally, Stuart is skeptical about the glyph that Pahl identifies as a Río Amarillo emblem-glyph; it and the purported Los Higos emblem-glyph may

103 *The south side of Structure 10L-11, with the Reviewing Stand at the base of the building, where it meets the floor of the West Court of the Acropolis.*

simply represent titles rather than the names of independent political entities.

Tenoned mosaic façade sculptures have been found by Seiichi Nakamura and his colleagues at several sites in the area of La Entrada, 60–70 km east of Copán.[17] Upon examining them one is struck by their similarities with the Copán mosaic sculptures. At one of the sites with sculptures – El Abra in the La Florida Valley – a tomb was found which contained an alabaster vase with glyphs carved in the tradition of fine carved ceramics at Copán. The text cites a Calendar Round date, the name of a local personage (presumably the occupant of the tomb), and, again, a relationship with the Copán king Yax Pac. Also in the tomb was a Copador cylinder vase (an obvious Copán import), and an Ulua polychrome vase (showing the strength of ties to central Honduras). All of these data indicate emulation of, and in some cases direct contact with, the court of Yax Pac on the part of the élites to the east of Copán.

Certainly the prominent display of the local ruler on Los Higos Stela 1 indicates a movement on the part of that site, at least, to political autonomy from Copán. Copán was losing its grip on the hinterlands, and the tribute that those areas had provided since the early days of the kingdom.

104 Pauahtun *head from the northeast corner of Structure* 10L-11. *This individual and his companion (ill. 105) represent the largest sculpted human figures found at Copán. Height 80 cm.*

105 Pauahtun *head fallen from the northwest corner of Structure* 10L-11. *This head tumbled all the way down to the bottom of the pyramidal base of the building (see ill. 25), and is consequently less well-preserved than its companion (ill. 104).*

The Acropolis under Yax Pac

What, then, was the response of Yax Pac, in terms of his own monuments on the Acropolis, his own symbols of power and authority? Yax Pac distinguished himself as a ruler not by erecting numerous stelae, or by constructing a Great Plaza to house them, or even a grandiloquent Hieroglyphic Stairway. Instead he sought to establish his authority through the massive renovation of two major Acropolis temple-pyramids: Structures 10L-11 and 10L-16. From the inscribed hieroglyphic bench on Structure 10L-21A, we know that he also built that structure on the east side of the Temple of Structure 10L-22 in AD 771, as his way of adding his own seal of approval to the still revered 'sacred mountain'.

Structure 10L-11 had always held an important place in the scheme of the site core of Copán, since before the time of Yax K'uk Mo'. Indeed, the 7th ruler had an exquisite 'head-variant' text inscribed on a hieroglyphic step leading into his own version of Structure 10L-11, which designated it as 'the lineage house of Yax K'uk Mo''. In *his* version of Structure 10L-11, Yax Pac sought to outdo all his ancestors, erecting a double-storied temple of unprecedented size and elaboration atop a substructure with more massive and impressive steps than anything else that had ever been attempted at Copán. There are over 3000 fragments of sculpture on the surface, probably another 3000 or so in the unexcavated parts of the substructure on its east, west and north sides.

The façade of this Temple 11 included the largest anthropomorphic figures ever carved in the Maya area, comprising two massive *Bacab* or *Pauahtun* figures, which adorned the northwest and northeast corners of the building. Proskouriakoff was the first to note that there were dozens of fragments of the body of what must have been a gigantic crocodile. The northern façade of Yax Pac's Structure 10L-11 represented an enormous version of the cosmogram depicted in the inner chamber of Structure 10L-22. Again, the message conveyed was that the ruler was the single individual who could control all the supernatural forces in the universe, and who was uniquely capable of providing for the well-being of his people. There were four doorways to the superstructure of the building, one at each of the cardinal points. On either side of each doorway was a panel of hieroglyphs, which give details of important rituals and political events during the early years of Yax Pac's reign. Such things as his accession date, two appearances of Venus as the Evening Star, a solar eclipse visible in the area on the date of its occurrence in AD 771, rituals that he apparently performed at one of the places cited on the Mat House, and other events, are recorded on the Temple 11 panels. Of particular delight to epigraphers is the fact that the glyphs on the right-hand panel at each doorway are carved in mirror image. This device was employed at other Classic Maya sites as well.

Just as Structure 10L-11's more public, north side was designed to mimic the content and message of the inner chamber of 18 Rabbit's Structure 10L-22, Yax

106 Structure 10L-16, in the heart of the Acropolis, during investigation and restoration by the Copán Acropolis Archaeological Project. Altar Q is visible at the foot of the central stairway.

Pac's other major Acropolis temple, Structure 10L-16, was designed to mimic Smoke Shell's Structure 10L-26. Straddling the East and West Courts, at the center of the Acropolis, Structure 10L-16 was the anchor of this important group of buildings. Again, numerous earlier versions of the building had come and gone, one of which was chosen by Butz' Chan as the appropriate place for the erection of his Stela P. Yax Pac's version of this temple was a rather gruesome affair, overtly sacrificial in content and presumably in purpose.

Its themes are identical to those of Structure 10L-26 and its temple annex (Structure 10L-230): ancestors as warriors (complete with shields and ropes) surrounded by Jaguar Tlaloc imagery and set off by a group of human skulls. (There are differences in format and layout, of course, but not in theme.)

On Structure 10L-26, Smoke Shell had created a Hieroglyphic Stairway and Temple as a medium for portraits of his royal ancestors. At Structure 10L-16 Yax Pac created Altar Q, a much more compact form of expressing the same thing. All 15 of his ancestors are portrayed on the sides of the altar, in chronological order, seated upon their name-glyphs, with Yax Pac himself shown on the date of his accession to the Copán throne. The idea seems to be that on the day he became king, Yax Pac symbolically communed with his royal ancestors, who gave him their blessing. And this same theme is portrayed on the carved step of the inner chamber of the Temple of Structure 10L-11. The message was clearly that Yax Pac derived his supernatural powers and secular authority from the fact that he is the legitimate heir.

As part of the commemoration of and subsequent rituals at Altar Q, Yax Pac placed an extraordinary offering in a sub-floor masonry crypt just east of the altar: 15 jaguars, one for each of his 15 royal ancestors. The jaguar was considered to be the intermediary between the world of the living and the world of the dead, and a protector and symbol for the Classic Maya royal houses. Even this stunning display of royal power – snaring 15 jaguars must have been no easy task – may reveal an underlying weakness: two of the cats were juveniles. The forests were retreating to the point that Yax Pac had to settle for less than prime specimens for his offering.

Whereas the portrait figures on Structure 10L-26 loom large and the Jaguar Tlaloc images form the backdrop, on Structure 10L-16 we find the reverse. Instead of ancestor portraits on the central axis of the stairway, there is the world's largest Jaguar Tlaloc visage, surrounded by ropes and standing over a group of large skulls (reminiscent of those which adorned Structure 10L-230). Instead of the two sizes of human figures in Structure 10L-26, there is only one size in Structure 10L-16; but there are six different types and sizes of Tlaloc heads, at least one of which was accompanied by ropes. Thus Structure 10L-16 appears to be the single most gory temple ever built in Copán, designed to inspire awe, respect, even fear, in those who saw it.

In AD 800 Yax Pac dedicated Temple 18, a small structure that is conspicuously separated from the great ritual plaza of the East Court. The most significant decoration on the building is on the two pairs of door jambs, whose sculpture is carved in shallow relief and not meant to be read from any great distance. The dates celebrated are not Period Endings, and the iconography is that of war and captive sacrifice, presented in a very blatant way. The diminutive size of the structure in comparison to previous Acropolis temples implies a lack of support for any grandiose building plans, even for what has been interpreted by some as Yax Pac's funerary temple. The explicit treatment of the ruler as a bearer of trophy heads would seem to indicate that he was attempting to reinforce his prowess as a warrior on his last known structure. We have noted that the emphasis on warrior iconography on Structure 10L-26 was borne not of strength, but of weakness, following the death of 18 Rabbit. Similarly, the characteristics of Yax Pac's last temple suggest that his power was in fact waning in the latter years of his reign.

Preamble to the collapse

The archaeological record indicates that Copán continued to grow in size and complexity throughout the reign of Yax Pac, satisfying the requirements of size, hierarchical structure, and organization of most definitions of the pre-industrial state. Indeed, the city grew to such a size that the agricultural carrying capacity of the Copán pocket's 24 sq. km was reached, and the population began to suffer from its own excesses. The alluvial bottomlands that made up the most fertile sectors of the valley were taken up in their majority by settlements, and the next best lands – the high river terraces and gently rolling foothills – were rapidly undergoing the same transformation. This left only the upper slopes, with thin layers of topsoil for extensive

107 The southwest portrait panel from Structure 10L-18, showing the 16th ruler brandishing a lance. Yax Pac's name-glyph appears directly in front of his right hand.

agriculture, causing detrimental long-term ecological consequences. Analysis of the human skeletal remains by Storey has shown that at the close of the 8th century, the majority of the population – both urban and rural – show signs of disease or malnutrition, or both.

Copán eventually became the victim of its own success, for after the carving of its last monument – Altar L – in AD 822, the centralized ruling apparatus collapsed, leaving the resident population of the valley to tend to their property and continue living in much the same way as before. The regional picture is one of demographic and political expansion of rival groups to the south and east, which may have been usurping clients and trading partners previously dominated by Copán. In short, grim tidings even for an energetic ruler such as Yax Pac.

On 9.19.0.0.0 (AD 810), the ruler of Quiriguá known as Jade Sky records an inscription on Structure 1-B-1 of his Acropolis that states that Yax Pac performed a 'scattering' ceremony there. This text would have us believe that the rulers of Copán and Quiriguá were able to set aside their previous differences, and band together at this late date. But the fact that no other inscribed monuments were erected at Quiriguá after the commemoration of this building suggests that Quiriguá, too, suffered a political crisis at this time.

The legacy of Yax Pac

In terms of political structure and cultural evolution, a number of insights into Classic Maya civilization are provided by Yax Pac's monuments. Perhaps most moving is Altar Q, which provides a fitting tribute to all the members of the Yax K'uk Mo' dynasty, and to the importance placed upon dynastic continuity. The 16th ruler is shown on the date of his accession to power, symbolically receiving the blessing of all his distinguished predecessors, and actually being presented with the baton of office by the founder himself. The need for the participation of other segments of society in the political order, however, is manifested in the great number of hieroglyphic and pictorial sculptures that were commemorated in the valley, in honor of the king's brothers – including the one who governed the area of the modern village – and of other noble lines. The placement in the Mat House of an inscribed text citing Yax Pac and his brothers Yahau Chan Ah Bac and Yax Kamlay bespeaks an effort to distribute authority for parts of the kingdom. When one considers that only eight lords are represented on the façades of the Mat House, when there were at least 20 sub-communities within (and several major towns outside) the Copán pocket, it becomes easy to understand why Yax Pac would want to delegate more authority to his closest collaborators.

At the same time, the long-term success of the expanding city bred a series of socio-economic problems with which the conservative political structure could not cope. The perpetuation of royal perquisites for the successive rulers, for their non-kingly descendants and cadet lineages, and the emulation of their life-style and status distinctions by other noble lines, resulted in a system that was top-heavy. Severe structural problems are posed by populations of élite men whose hereditary positions permit them to rise to positions of power in societies where there are very few such positions.[18] The strong dependence on the charisma and actions of the Classic Maya ruler, and the relatively underdeveloped nature of hierarchical institutions divorced from kinship lines, meant that it was difficult to accommodate the perceived needs and rival claims of the competing non-kingly factions of Maya city-states. The innovative approaches to this problem devised and implemented by Yax Pac indicate a willingness (arguably born of need) to engage in power-sharing with important members of Late Classic Copán society. Unfortunately his efforts, largely based upon his own prestige and performance of 'scattering' and house dedication rituals for his subordinates, were not sufficiently institutionalized to fend off the forces that led to the demise of dynastic power at Copán.

CHAPTER NINE

THE POLITICAL COLLAPSE AND ITS AFTERMATH

It is not enough to ask why it fell; why it failed to revive is an integral part of the puzzle.[1]

The question of the 'Classic Maya collapse' at Copán

Perhaps no other question in the field of New World archaeology has attracted as much scholarly and popular attention as the causes of the collapse of Classic Maya civilization. The process in question is hardly unique to the Maya, but perhaps because of the encroachment of tropical rainforest on the Classic period centers, and the physical disappearance of these now 'lost cities', their case has been emphasized and to a degree mystified by numerous writers. The School of American Research symposium organized by Patrick Culbert in the early 1970s served to demystify the issue by developing an explicit model for the collapse, and charting areas for further data gathering and comparative research.[2] The consensus of the symposium was that internal problems, particularly those related to what Culbert calls 'ecological overshoot' and the increasingly parasitic role of the élite, were the primary causes for the social, political, and demographic collapse of the southern lowland Maya city-states in the 9th century AD. Demitri Shimkin pointed out the importance of communicable diseases in tropical forest urban settings, and showed the utility of comparing the Maya case with those of other cultures from similar environments, particularly in Southeast Asia.[3] Others in the symposium emphasized the role of the disruption of long-established trade routes by outsiders as a contributing factor in the internal failures of the system.

In the case of Copán, dramatic increases in population size through the 7th and 8th centuries AD placed increasing stress on both the socio-political system and on the environment. Here we will examine the manner in which the increasingly interdependent politico-economic system failed, and the evidence for long-term ecological deterioration, population decline, and the eventual abandonment of the area. By the end of PAC I in 1979, we had managed to work out what the major factors of the decline were, but greatly telescoped the amount of time in which they took place. Fortunately, some of us were at least cautious enough at that time to bemoan the 'lack of a refined ceramic chronology for the final years of the Late Classic Coner phase'.[4]

In the intervening years William Sanders, David Webster, and their students have continued work on the Coner-phase settlements and on the environmental history of the valley – using obsidian hydration dating rather than ceramic chronology. Their work has unequivocally demonstrated a much longer process than the 'rapid devolution' that I and other PAC I researchers had posited. Now when one talks of the Copán 'collapse' there are three facets to consider: the decentralization of power during the 8th and early 9th centuries AD; the political collapse of Copán kingship in AD 822; and the demographic decline of the supporting population and ecological deterioration of the Copán Valley (which apparently continued to be occupied until as late as AD 1200).[5]

In the previous chapter, we noted that the study of settlement patterns has shown a great degree of nucleation and population density in the Copán pocket. It was argued that the population had reached a state level of organization, and numbers considerably in excess of those that could be supported by the agricultural lands not taken up by settlements in the Copán pocket itself. This undoubtedly resulted in increasing competition among the Copanecs themselves, and arguably to some rather desperate innovations on the part of king Yax Pac to keep the social fabric united.

Social stratification in the Coner phase was becoming well marked by architecture. The volume of construction, as well as elaboration, of superstructures and paved surfaces appears to be our best evidence for discerning social status. Even in graves, the architecture probably reflects social status. Burials range from simple graves, to graves with capstone(s), to cists, to crypts with capstones, to a few cases of vaulted crypts with capstones. Elaborate ceramic and jade offerings, on the other hand, are not as common – even in the richer graves – as they were in the earlier Acbi phase. Status appears to have been measured in terms of labor and in the monumental things labor could accomplish, rather than in showy objects. By implication the system had become labor exploitative, with the upper classes marshaling the energy of their lower-class vassals to build architectural monuments in their honor.

This system has its most obvious reflection in the Principal Group, but the same pattern is replicated down through the social ranks in the remainder of the valley, as observable in the settlement site typology: it was obviously preferable to have a larger abode than one's contemporaries. Stratification thus produced non-egalitarian and exploitative behavior, and highly visible physical and symbolic manifestations of it, serving to widen the gap between the élite and their less fortunate contemporaries. Add to this the possibility of intra-societal conflicts based on ethnic affiliations, and the level of internal conflict, during a time of economic shortfalls and communicable diseases, would have been raised to an intense pitch.

But who might have been the challengers to Yax Pac in the latter years of his reign? Eric Thompson long championed the role of peasant revolts, and many researchers see his hypothesis as still valid.[6] Higher up on the social ladder, the Maya chronicles of 16th-century Yucatán, and comparative material from many other parts of the globe, allow for the possibility that a rival lineage or series of rival lineages and allied factions might have been involved in the overthrow of the political order. Farther afield, it is quite possible that rival polities in the southeastern periphery were involved. Some of the towns developing in central Honduras and western El Salvador had dense populations, and were probably developing the social complexity and political centralization that characterize such settlements. Certainly the entire area was experiencing a notable demographic build-up, and any one of a number of towns, resentful of Copán's dominant status, could have mounted a military threat to the Copán rulership.

The nobles' revolt

It has long been the author's position that competition between noble lines, or between noble lines and the Copán dynasty, probably contributed heavily to the breakdown of the kingdom. Instead of a peasant revolt, I believe that in Copán – and quite possibly at many of the other long-established Classic-period cities – there was a nobles' revolt. A parallel example is known for the city of Mayapán in northern Yucatán, where in the Late Postclassic period tensions among rival factions led to the unseating of an unpopular lineage head:

And this they did, killing at the same time all his sons, except one who was absent. They sacked his house and took away the lands which he had in cacao and in other fruits, saying that they paid themselves for what he had taken from them. The quarrels between the Cocoms, who said that they had been unjustly expelled, and the Xius lasted so long, that after they had lived in that city for more than five hundred years, they abandoned it and left it in solitude, each party returning to his own country.[7]

The particulars of such inter-élite conflicts may be very difficult to ascertain from non-historical evidence, and it will certainly be difficult to determine what the nature and intensity of lineage rivalry in Copán was. However, it seems that the written records do imply tension within the power politics at the top of the system. If Yax Pac were indeed caught up in disputes among the then powerful noble families in Copán, that would explain why so much effort was expended to produce monuments for them in the valley. The state's lifeline was its tribute, large portions of which were funneled through the largest, oldest, and most powerful lineages. The heads of each of these important noble lines must perforce have been well satisfied by their relationship with the ruler if the system were to prosper; and the bench thrones and building façades were one highly visible, exclusive, and rather expensive symbolic gesture which Yax Pac could grant through his offices. In the last chapter we noted that a non-royal 'courtier' office was created for the noble lineage heads who lived in Sepulturas Structures CV 43-A and 9N-82. Further excavations in other Type 3 and 4 sites in the valley may reveal that Yax Pac created similar offices for their occupants.

Here it is important to note that obsidian hydration dating has shown that the élite Type 4 residential compounds of the Copán pocket continued to be

108 Stela 11, showing a posthumous portrait of the 16th ruler, Yax Pac. The smoking axe in his forehead indicates his apotheosis, and he stands on a shell symbolic of the Underworld.

109 (Right) Altar L of Copán. On the completed, south side, U Cit Tok sits to the left of the accession date – as did the founder Yax K'uk Mo' on Altar Q – and Yax Pac sits on the right. The carving on the north side was never completed.

built and occupied right through the 9th century, and in some cases into the 10th century, indicating that the families residing there had sufficient lands and sources of wealth of their own to survive the political collapse without major problems.[8] Considering the small number of positions available, even allowing for the creation of a few new 'symbolic' public offices by Yax Pac, against the large numbers of élite males who would have considered themselves candidates for them, it must have been virtually impossible for the king to please all of them, all of the time.

Another important possible source of disruption in the political system was inter-ethnic conflict. As noted, there is evidence for at least some non-Maya occupants at Copán in the 8th and 9th centuries in the Sepulturas residential ward. Their numbers, distribution, and social position cannot be accurately determined by our present evidence, and the possibility of factionalism and social undercurrents are obviously difficult to estimate with precision. Nonetheless, when compared to 16th-century accounts there is little doubt that they were important elements in historical processes. In personal communica-

tions, William Sanders has suggested to me that non-Maya groups may have helped Cauac Sky of Quiriguá defeat 18 Rabbit, and such short-lived alliances could have been just as troublesome to 18 Rabbit's successors.

The last inscribed monuments in the Principal Group

Whatever the nature and source of the social conflicts leading to the political collapse of the Copán state, their effect was undeniable. On Stela 11, we see a very late portrait of Yax Pac, placed in a small, crudely carved cylindrical stone placed at the base of Structure 10L-18. On his forehead is shown a smoking axe, symbolic of his apotheosis as God K, the patron of Maya kings and royal lineages. He stands atop a shell, symbolic of the watery Underworld where he resided after death. Although there is no death date on Stela 11, the Calendar Round date '8 Ahau' appears, which in all likelihood refers to the Period Ending 9.19.10.0.0 8 Ahau 8 Xul, or AD 820. We may reliably infer that by this date Yax Pac (by then almost certainly in his seventies) had died. The epigraphers have noted that the Stela 11 text also states that the founder's house (the Yax K'uk Mo' dynasty) ended with Yax Pac.

Stela 11's death imagery and its position next to Temple 18 led Baudez and his colleagues in PAC I to conclude that this building was constructed to house his remains.[9] Yax Pac's name appears next to two of the portraits on the four panels adorning the door jambs of the outer and inner chambers of the structure; and there was a vaulted tomb chamber built into the substructure, beneath the floor of the inner room of the building. The tomb itself had been looted in ancient times, the grave robbers leaving only a few scattered fragments of human bones, a broken jade bead, and an incised alabaster vase fragment in their wake. The head of the southwest portrait panel was found by Sheree Lane and the author in investigations at Ballcourt B (some 320 m southwest of Temple 18), in an area where numerous potsherds of Plumbate ware (dated to the 9th century AD), and green obsidian (frequently found with Plumbate pottery at this time in the southern Maya area) were found. It seems quite likely that Yax Pac's tomb was looted, and his funerary temple ransacked, sometime in the century after his death. Indeed, Stela 11 itself was found broken in half.

Given this turn of events, Copán Altar L takes on added interest. Placed on top of the terrace forming the northern limit of the final version of Ballcourt A, this rectangular altar has the distinction of being the only one never finished: the front (south) side is carved, and the carving on the back (north) side was started, but not completed. On the top, east, and west sides the carving was never even started. The front side has a single column of three glyphs placed centrally between two seated personages. The text reads '3 Chicchan 3 Uo, chumwan', which has been read by Nikolai Grube and Linda Schele as 9.19.11.14.5 3 Chicchan 3 Uo, 'seating of the ruler' (10 February AD 822). The figure on the viewer's right is Yax Pac, identifiable by the name-glyph beneath him and by the beard he wears in death (just as he is shown on Stela 11).

This is certainly not Yax Pac's accession date – 6 Caban 10 Mol, as recorded and still visible on numerous monuments and stone incense burners throughout the city – so the seating reference on Altar L must relate to the figure on the left. This figure is seated upon two glyphs which Grube and Schele read as 'U Cit Tok'' (Patron of Flint), and identified by them as a 17th ruler of Copán. The epigraphers have further noted that U Cit Tok' sits in a position similar to that occupied by the dynasty founder Yax K'uk Mo' on Altar Q. Given that Stela 11 states that the old dynasty ended with the death of Yax Pac, this position is the proper one for a new 'founder'.

Accepting these readings and conclusions of a very short and incomplete text as correct, it nevertheless seems unlikely that U Cit Tok' ever attained the level of support from the populace commensurate with a true ruler. The fact that the carving of the altar which would have served as his accession monument was never completed shows a lack of long-term backing, to say the least. Also telling in this regard is that this small monument was carved in a previously built public place. This hardly constitutes a convincing show of popular support when compared with the massive Temple 11, constructed by Yax Pac after his accession.

Finally, why is it that over a year passed between the death of Yax Pac and the purported accession of U Cit Tok'? This is the longest known interregnum at Copán, and does not bespeak political continuity in the waning years of the kingdom. Could he be a valley noble whose claims to greatness were not supported by his peers? I consider this individual to be a somewhat tragic figure, the man who tried to assume the Copán throne when lineage and political factionalism prevented unification under a new royal house. In one of those telling ironies of history, the new dynasty which he proclaimed on his accession altar ended with its first member.

Perspectives from the valley

But what of the people living throughout the valley? Previously, it was thought that deteriorating environmental conditions caused them to abandon their homesteads within two or three generations of the collapse of centralized rule. But now, the refined dating made possible through the obsidian hydration technique renders this conclusion premature, and shows that the population in the Copán pocket remained there for over a century after U Cit Tok's ill-fated attempts to take over the throne. In fact, most of the sites in the Las Sepulturas ward continued to be occupied, and in most tested cases were actually extended or altered until the end of the 10th century AD. The Type 4 site of Group 9N-8 is an excellent example, with major buildings added to the House of the Bacabs.[10]

But one major population shift shown by the Pennsylvania State settlement surveys began in the 9th century, when large numbers of people moved out of the Copán pocket itself: in the 8th century about 90 percent of the population lived in the pocket, but by the end of the 9th century 22–37 percent lived outside the pocket in what Sanders and his colleagues refer to as the periphery.[11] Many people seem to have moved out of the El Bosque residential ward just west of the Main Group. By the same token, Sanders estimates that from AD 850 to 925 the population of the rural Copán pocket dropped from 10,000 to 5000.

There seem to have been powerful incentives for moving from the Copán pocket in the half-century after the collapse of centralized rule. The likely cause of this movement must have been a lack of cultivable fields. Within the Copán pocket the evidence of ceramics and sculptures suggests that there were cacao orchards in the bottomlands, and possibly other tree crops and garden plots. Similarly, the infield–outfield system proposed by Robert Netting and Sanders (where the produce of small intensively cultivated garden plots close to the house was supplemented by other crops raised in extensive fields at some distance from the home) seems to be supported by the Copán evidence. In the Copán Valley, the densely-settled urban core lacked areas large enough for extensive cultivation, but the foothills and intra-montane areas away from the core show evidence of terracing, water catchment basins, and even a possible dam, implying the intensification of agriculture.[12] However, in the long run this strategy could not keep up with the demands of a population of 20,000 people, and the landscape was dramatically altered.

In the last chapter we noted that extensive areas of the foothills in the Copán pocket were cleared of forest, then cultivated, and finally also taken up by residential quarters. By the middle of the 9th century, forest clearing was extended higher up, as people sought new lands for farming, and the need for wood itself increased with the expanding population. Some time ago I hypothesized that drastic clearing of the foothills in the Late Classic resulted in a marked loss of topsoil through erosion.[13] Such erosion would have resulted both from the loss of ground cover and from intensification of agricultural practices, particularly short fallow or non-fallow cycles and monocropping in maize, a nitrogen-demanding crop. A similar sequence of clearing and erosion is occurring in certain parts of the Copán pocket today, as a new cycle of demographic pressure on the land makes itself felt. The upper slopes in the Titichón and Buenavista area south of the river are not only losing their best topsoil as a result of extensive clearing and short fallow cycles, but they are also depositing layers of poorer, acidic soils on the lower foothills and the bottom-lands zones below, through runoff during the rainy season. This results not only in the accumulation of unwanted sediments on top of optimum soils, but also in undesirable water retention, causing waterlogging of fields and insect infestation in the maize crop. Such a sequence would result in the eventual degradation or even ruination of all three physiographic zones: upper slopes, lower foothills and high river terrace, and prime bottomlands.

Of course, short fallow cycles in any zone of the pocket would have been counterproductive in the long run, regardless of the erosion risk, given the nitrogen requirements of maize. Intensification techniques without adequate regeneration and nutrient replacement methods would have resulted in massive soil exhaustion, precisely when the most people needed to be fed, and the most pressure existed to keep them all fed well. For the moment, however, all the evidence supports the hypothesis that deforestation and over-cultivation alone caused soil exhaustion and loss.

The whole question of deforestation, and its causes and effects, has been discussed recently by Elliot Abrams and David Rue.[14] The forest, particularly pine forest, would have been exploited for firewood and charcoal, for construction material, and for the production of lime. Given the population figures cited above, the costs of clearing, and the basic assumption that Copanec households would attempt to exploit the closer wood resources intensively, Abrams and Rue estimate that between AD 600 and 800 about 56 sq. km of pine forest would have been removed. This would constitute a band 2.3 km wide on each side of the agricultural land in the Copán pocket, for its entire east–west length of 12 km. They note that in studies of clearing and erosion patterns in modern-day central Honduras, the removal of pine forest increases the erosion rate of soils by about 25 percent over the natural process.

We must also note that one of the most damaging long-term effects of deforestation is climatic instability, including the long-term loss of rainfall. This cycle of clearing, intensive agriculture, and eventual ecological destruction has occurred in numerous hearths of 'advanced civilizations' in the history of the globe, perhaps the most dramatic example being the Mesopotamian plain, now a sterile desert. The present-day cycle of clearing in the Copán Valley has reduced the ground cover quite drastically, when compared to Stephens' descriptions in 1839 and the unpublished photographs of the valley taken by the Peabody Museum Expedition of the 1890s. In fact, many of the oldest villagers complain of there being much less rain now than when they were younger. Further ecological studies may therefore show that variation in and decline of precipitation followed deforestation during the 9th and 10th centuries, resulting in further disruption of agriculture.

Obviously, all of these cultural shifts and resulting environmental degradations had severe repercussions on the human population. Nutritional standards appear to have deteriorated progressively through the later Coner phase, both from agricultural difficulties, and possibly from the spread of communicable diseases. Due to social ranking we may be confident that the lower classes were the first to suffer from this situation, by reductions in both quantity and variety of foodstuffs.[15] The effects on the middle and upper strata of Copanec society are harder to gauge. There are indications that even the élite sites such as Group 9N-8 suffered health crises. Excavations here produced not only large numbers of infant burials, but also numerous 10- to 16-year-old individuals. This is the age-group least susceptible to death under normal conditions, indicating that there were severe diseases and possibly nutritional problems even in the upper-class population.[16]

The demographic decline following the dissolution of centralized rule was clearly a protracted one, tied to long-term environmental degradation. The evidence of environmental destruction helps us answer the question posed at the beginning of this chapter: why was there no recovery? First, the environment itself was depleted to the point that urban concentrations were not feasible. Second, the conflicts and stresses that prevailed during the last century of dynastic rule at Copán militated against any one faction attempting to re-establish the centralized system, at least within the confines of the Copán pocket. There, the Principal Group and its falling monuments stood witness to the failures, as well as to the successes, of the Classic Maya way of life.

Urbanization and the Classic Maya order

In the end, one can argue that both the nucleated settlement pattern and the political and ideological sub-systems of Maya states worked against long-term success. In Copán, inter-lineage competition reached extremes in the final decades of the 8th century, physically manifested in the different heights, bulks, and elaborations of lineage compound architecture. This competition, moreover, extended beyond the boundaries of the city-state to the regional level, as between Copán and Quiriguá. The larger question, posed long ago by Willey and Shimkin, is why the turbulence of the Late Classic period did not lead to the emergence of a unified state.[17] Why did the Maya not take the next step in the ladder of political evolution, to create one state, or several regional states, which might have unified their cities within one system?

One possible answer has been put forward by Arthur Demarest, who, like Shimkin, looked to Southeast Asian cultures for analogies to the Maya case.

Demarest cites the work of the socio-cultural anthropologist Stanley Tambiah, who defined a series of competing segmentary state systems as 'pulsating galactic polities'.[18] These political entities are characterized by weak control over the land and its products, with political authority based more on the charismatic leadership of the ruler, and on the frequency and effectiveness of ritual displays of concern for his subjects, than on real institutionalized power. This combination results in a highly volatile political landscape, with competing towns constantly waxing and waning according to the political fortunes and prestige of their individual rulers. This causes a 'pulsating' effect, with one polity growing as another one recedes in size and importance. Such a political system has so many inherent structural weaknesses that political unification under a single royal house is extremely difficult.

Closer to home, Joyce Marcus has recently proposed a 'dynamic model' for explaining the cycles of centralization and decentralization in the Maya lowlands, based on an analysis of ethnohistoric documents regarding the 16th- and 17th-century Maya, and the ethnohistoric, epigraphic, and archaeological information for the Postclassic- and Classic-period Maya.[19] Marcus believes that the Maya were able to form large regional states based on the concept of *mul tepal* or 'joint rule'. In her view, these large states were organized along quadripartite and four-tiered hierarchical lines. Mayapán and Chichén Itzá were examples of *mul tepal* from the Postclassic period, and (according to 18 Rabbit in the text of the south side of Copán Stela A) Copán, Tikal, Calakmul, and Palenque were examples from the Classic period, in AD 731. The centers of these large polities ruled over secondary centers, tertiary centers, and villages. Significantly, the primary centers never warred with each other, if we are to believe the records carved in stone. The problems, according to Marcus, were always with the secondary centers. Faced with the question of whether it was better to be a part of the system of joint rule and to have greater stability (at the cost of their autonomy), or to be independent from this system and enjoy greater autonomy (at the cost of increased warfare), the different towns and lineages were constantly in danger of breaking their alliances with each other. The lords of the secondary centers, who controlled the resources and manpower of large areas, were the weak link in the whole hierarchy. When they broke away from the capital – as Quiriguá did from Copán in AD 738 – they contributed to the dissolution of joint rule, and the reversion to a political landscape of autonomous provinces. In this model, unification and breakdown went on continuously from at least AD 534 to the Spanish Conquest, which accounts for the fluid nature of political relations between centers during this period.[20]

The lack of political unification may have its causes both in the material world (with tremendous transport and logistics problems hindering large-scale unification in the Maya lowlands), and in the social and religious constructs of Maya culture. Copán and virtually all other Classic Maya centers show a cultural system which was simply not well-adapted to urbanism or to empire-building. Unlike the compartmentalization of artisans and foreign groups into distinctive residential units, as at Teotihuacan and Tenochtitlan in Central Mexico, Maya residential patterns were kin-based, or kin-and-client based, such as at Group 9N-8 at Copán. Maya society in general, to the end of the Classic period and beyond, was organized along kinship lines, a trait which many anthropologists would use to deny that it reached state level. Even though the *popol na* (Mat House or 'Community House') represented in Structure 10L-22A was used by the last three Copán kings to bring in representatives from the various sub-divisions of their domain, and perhaps to serve as a means of holding them responsible for the future of the kingdom and the people, this strategy was not enough to overcome the parasitic tendencies of the land-holding élites in the valley.

The Classic Maya centers, as 'regal-ritual' cities – or petty kingdoms, if you will – waxed and waned in tandem with the political fortunes of the élite lineages at the top of the social pyramid. The religious and political sub-systems, focused on ancestor worship and ruler exaltation, did not provide an integrating mechanism sufficiently powerful to transcend the local rivalries, or the considerable obstacles to unification presented by the environment and technology of ancient Mesoamerica. Nevertheless the collective efforts of the Maya, the monumental fruits of their labors, and the roles of kings and commoners alike in the history of their people, continue to fascinate and perplex students of human culture the world over.

Bibliography

BAUDEZ, CLAUDE F. (ed.) *Introduccíon a la Arqueologia de Copan* (3 vols.), Secretaria de Estado en el Despacho de Cultura y Turismo, Tegucigalpa, Honduras, 1983.

COE, MICHAEL D. *The Maya Scribe and His World*. The Grolier Club, New York, 1973.

Copán Mosaics Project and Instituto Hondureño de Antropología e Historia, *The Copán Notes*, available through Kinko's Copies, 2914 Medical Arts St., Austin, Texas, 1985–1991.

CULBERT, T. PATRICK (ed.) *The Classic Maya Collapse*, University of New Mexico Press, Albuquerque, 1973.

FASH, WILLIAM L. 'Deducing Social Organization from Classic Maya Settlement Patterns: A Case Study from the Copan Valley'. In *Civilization in the Ancient Americas: Essays in Honor of Gordon R. Willey*, University of New Mexico Press, Albuquerque, 1983.

GORDON, GEORGE B. *The Hieroglyphic Stairway, Ruins of Copán*, Memoirs of the Peabody Museum of American Archaeology and Ethnology, Vol. 1(4), Harvard University Press, Cambridge, Mass., 1902.

LONGYEAR, JOHN. *Copan Ceramics: A Study of Southeastern Maya Pottery*, Carnegie Institution of Washington (Publication 597), Washington, D.C., 1952.

MARCUS, JOYCE. *Emblem and State in the Classic Maya Lowlands*, Dumbarton Oaks Research Library and Collection, Washington, D.C., 1976.

MAUDSLAY, ALFRED P. *Biologia Centrali-Americana: Archaeology* (5 vols.), Dulau and Co, London, 1889–1902. (Reprint edition, Milparton Publishing Co., 1974.)

MORLEY, SYLVANUS G. *The Inscriptions at Copan*, Carnegie Institution of Washington (Publication 219), Washington, D.C., 1920.

PROSKOURIAKOFF, TATIANA. *An Album of Classic Maya Architecture*, Carnegie Institution of Washington (Publication 558), Washington, D.C., 1946. (Reprint edition, University of Oklahoma Press, 1963.)

ROBICSEK, FRANCIS. *Copán: Home of the Mayan Gods*, Museum of the American Indian, New York, 1972.

SANDERS, WILLIAM T. (ed.) *Excavaciones en el Area Urbana de Copan* (Vol. 1), Instituto Hondureño de Antropología e Historia, Tegucigalpa, Honduras, 1986.

SCHELE, LINDA, and DAVID FREIDEL. *A Forest of Kings: The Untold Story of the Ancient Maya*, William Morrow and Co., New York, 1990.

SHARER, ROBERT J. *Quirigua. A Classic Maya Center and its Sculptures*, Carolina Academic Press, Durham, 1990.

STEPHENS, JOHN L. *Incidents of Travel in Central America, Chiapas, and Yucatan*, Harper and Brothers, New York, 1841. (Reprint edition, Dover Publications, New York, 1969.)

TOZZER, ALFRED M. *Landa's Relacion de las Cosas de Yucatan*, Papers of the Peabody Museum of American Archaeology and Ethnology, Harvard University (Vol. 18), Cambridge, Mass., 1941.

WEBSTER, DAVID (ed.) *The House of the Bacabs*, Dumbarton Oaks Research Library and Collections, Washington, D.C., 1989.

WILLEY, GORDON R., RICHARD M. LEVENTHAL, and WILLIAM L. FASH. 'Maya Settlement in the Copan Valley'. *Archaeology*, 31(4), 1978, pp. 32–43.

Notes to the text

Chapter 1 *(pp. 9–34)*
1 Stephens 1841:105.
2 Morley 1920:431.
3 The idea that Altar Q portrayed the rulers, with each seated upon his name-glyph, was first suggested by Joyce Marcus (1976).
4 Morley 1920:14.
5 In his 1974 book, *Copán: Home of the Mayan Gods*, Francis Robicsek suggested that Copán was considered the 'place of the bats', and that the Copanecs may have considered themselves 'the bat people'. This suggestion was seconded by Joyce Marcus in her book *Emblem and State in the Classic Maya Lowlands* (1976:124). In *Deciphering the Maya Script* (1976:208), David Kelley followed up on the earlier writings of Thomas Barthel, and suggested that the bat (*zotz*) sign could in fact be read as a homonym of a highland Mayan word for 'clouds', and that the Copán emblem-glyph was to be read as 'place of the clouds'. More recently, Nikolai Grube read the bat sign as phonetic *xu*, and since the cauac infix is read *ku* in Landa's 'alphabet' of signs, and David Stuart reads the other infix as phonetic *pi*, Matthew Looper has suggested that the main sign of the Copán emblem-glyph was read *xukpi* (a generic term for 'birds'; *Copán Notes* 96), i.e. 'place of the birds'.
6 Proskouriakoff 1963:31.

Chapter 2 *(pp. 35–46)*
1 Marcus 1976:126.
2 Turner II, B.L., William Johnson, Gail Mahood, Frederick M. Wiseman, B.L. Turner, and Jackie Poole, 1983, 'Habitat y Agricultura en la Region de Copan', in *Introduccion a la Arqueología de Copan*, Baudez (Vol. 1):42.
3 Turner *et al* 1983:55–66.
4 Turner *et al* 1983:85.
5 Carneiro, Robert L., 1970, 'A Theory on the Origin of the State', *Science* 69:733–738.
6 Rue, David, 1987, 'Early Agriculture and Early Postclassic Maya Occupation in Western Honduras', *Nature* 326 (6110):285–286.

Chapter 3 *(pp. 47–62)*
1 Maudslay 1889–1902 (Vol. 5):12.
2 García de Palacio, in Morley 1920:541.

3 García de Palacio, in Morley 1920:542.
4 García de Palacio, in Morley 1920:542.
5 Stephens 1841:128. Less well known is the fact that the Honduran government recovered the title to the ruins and passed legislation for their protection within five years of Stephens' purchase.
6 Graham, Ian 1976.
7 Maudslay 1889–1902 (Vol. 5):16.
8 Gordon 1902.
9 Stuart, George, 1988, 'New Light on the Maya', pp. 204–217.
10 Morley 1920:399.
11 Morley 1920:402.
12 Willey, Gordon R. and Richard M. Leventhal, 1979, 'Prehistoric Settlement Patterns in the Copan Valley, Honduras', in *Mesoamerican Archaeology: New Approaches*, Norman Hammond and Gordon Willey (eds.), pp. 75–102.
13 Sanders 1986. The investigators who pursued these topics in their doctoral dissertations were David Rue (pollen analysis and vegetational history); Elliot Abrams (energetics of construction); John Wingard (soils analysis); Mary Spink (ground stone); Julia Hendon (structure function); Andrea Gerstle (ethnicity); Melissa Diamanti (activity areas); John Mallory (lithic analysis); AnnCorinne Freter (obsidian hydration and the dating of the valley settlements); and Stephen Whittington (skeletal analysis). Rebecca Storey has been conducting a more in-depth analysis of the human skeletal remains from Copán and Salitron Viejo (central Honduras).
14 Webster, David and Elliot Abrams, 1983, 'An Elite Compound at Copan, Honduras', *Journal of Field Archaeology*, 10:285–296.

Chapter 4 *(pp. 63–76)*
1 Fash, William L., 1983b, 'Reconocimiento y Excavaciones en el Valle', in Baudez Vol. 1.
2 Willey and Leventhal 1979. The Group numbers were adapted from the map system employed at Tikal, Dzibilchaltún, and other Maya sites due to the facility with which the site can be localized on the overall map using the grid coordinates (e.g. '9N', '10L', etc.).
3 Gordon, George B., 1898, *Caverns of Copan, Honduras: Report on Explorations by the Museum, 1896–1897*, Vol. 1 (5):137–148.

4 Pyne, Nanette, 1976, 'The Fire-Serpent and Were-Jaguar in Formative Oaxaca: A Contingency Table Analysis', in *The Early Mesoamerican Village*, Kent V. Flannery (ed.).

5 Cheek, Charles, 1983, 'Excavaciones en la Plaza Principal', in *Introducción a la Arqueología de Copán*, Baudez (Vol. 1):191–290.

6 Schele, Linda and David Freidel, 1989, 'Kingship in the Late Preclassic Maya Lowlands: The Instruments and Places of Ritual Power', *American Anthropologist* 90:547–567.

7 Fash, William L. and David S. Stuart, 1991, 'Dynastic History and Cultural Evolution at Copán, Honduras', in *Classic Maya Political History: Archaeological and Hieroglyphic Evidence*, T. Patrick Culbert (ed.).

Chapter 5 *(pp. 77–114)*

1 Definitions vary widely, most notably regarding the requisite size of the population and the degree to which organizational structures must be divorced from kinship lines. To many, the latter stricture is a bias in Western thinking that is not appropriate for the analysis of many pre-industrial societies.

2 Pendergast, David M., 1988, 'Lamanai Stela 9: The Archaeological Context', *Research Reports on Ancient Maya Writing*, Number 20.

3 Stuart, David and Linda Schele, 1986, 'Yax-K'uk-Mo', the Founder of the Lineage of Copán', *Copán Notes*, Number 6; Stuart, David, Nikolai Grube, Linda Schele, and Floyd Lounsbury, 1989, 'Stela 63, A New Monument from Copán', *Copán Notes*, Number 56.

4 Personal communication, 1987.

5 Cogolludo, D. López de, 1688, *Historia de Yucatán*, Madrid, p. 186.

6 *Copán Notes* Numbers 94 and 95.

7 Baudez (Vol. 2):190.

8 Stuart, David, Nikolai Grube *et al*, 1989.

9 Fash 1983b:229–469.

10 Fash 1983b:445.

11 Landa, Diego de, in Tozzer 1941:130.

12 Rathje, William, 1971, 'Lowland Classic Maya Socio-Political Organization: Degree and Form in Time and Space', unpublished PhD dissertation, Harvard University.

13 Stromsvik, Gustav, 1952, 'The Ball Courts at Copán, with Notes on Courts at La Union, Quirigua, San Pedro Pinula, and Ascension Mita', in *Carnegie Institution Publication 596*.

14 Agurcia Fasquelle, Ricardo and William L. Fash, April 1991, 'Maya Artistry Unearthed', *National Geographic*.

15 Spinden, Herbert J., 1913, *A Study of Maya Art: Its Subject Matter and Historical Development*, Vol. 6.

16 Morley 1920:133.

17 Proskouriakoff, Tatiana, 1973, 'The Hand-grasping-fish and Associated Glyphs on Classic Maya Monuments', in *Mesoamerican Writing Systems: A Conference at Dumbarton Oaks, October 30th and 31st, 1971*, Elizabeth Benton (ed.), pp. 165–178.

18 This burial was found by Richard Williamson and the author during the tunneling operations in 1989 (see *National Geographic*, Vol. 176 (4), October 1989, 'Copán, A Royal Tomb Discovered').

19 Fash, William L., 1983d, 'Maya State Formation: A Case Study and its Implications', unpublished PhD dissertation (Vol. 1):225–226.

Chapter 6 *(pp. 115–137)*

1 Proskouriakoff 1963:31.

2 Webster, David (ed.) 1989.

3 Coe, Michael D., 1976, 'Supernatural Patrons of Maya Scribes and Artists', in *Social Process in Maya Prehistory: Essays in Honor of Sir Eric Thompson*, Norman Hammond, (ed.), pp. 327–396.

4 Schele, Linda, 1987, 'A Possible Death Date for Smoke-Imix-God K', *Copán Notes*, Number 26. The recent decipherment of the title read *itz'at* ('learned man', 'sage', 'man of letters'), and its presence at the sites of Tortuguero, Piedras Negras, and Copán, indicates that an office of scribe existed in the Classic period, just as it did at the time of the Spanish conquest. As noted in the last chapter, both the 3rd and 4th rulers of Copán cited this title in their names.

5 Schele, Linda and Mary Ellen Miller, 1986, *The Blood of Kings: Dynasty and Ritual in Maya Art*, p. 154.

6 Fash, Barbara, and William L. Fash (in press), 'Copán Temple 20 and the House of Bats', in *Sixth Round Table of Palenque*, Merle Greene Robertson (ed.).

7 Personal communications, 1990. The author does not mean to imply that there was no disjunction between earlier and later forms of political organization among the Maya, or earlier and later political symbolism (including the use and meaning of the mat symbol); there almost certainly was. In this vein, it should be noted that the office of *batab* documented by Roys and others may be the one represented by the figures displayed on Copán Structure 10L-22A, or perhaps the office had some altogether different name. The name of the office is of less concern here than the way in which the representatives were conceived (associated with the mat of rulership), and what their duties and obligations were.

8 We should also leave open the possibility that the glyphs refer to the names of noble lineages, or to the supernatural patrons of those lineages.

9 Roys, Ralph, 1939, *The Titles of Ebtún*, Carnegie Institution Publication 505, p. 44.

10 David Stuart noted that the 9 Ahau glyph was combined (or 'conflated', as epigraphers say) with the T.537 *na* ('house') glyph. This means that the glyph in fact says '9 Ahau house', and may refer to the number of lords that convened there (8 representatives, plus the king). However, the architectural, stratigraphic, and epigraphic evidence show that the 9.15.15.0.0 date corresponds well with the time of the construction of

Structure 10L-22A, so it may be that the Maya combined both meanings in a single glyph: the Mat House of the 9 lords (*ahau*), the Mat House built on the day 9 Ahau.

11 Marcus 1976; Mathews, Peter, and John S. Justeson, 1984, 'Patterns of Sign Substitution in Mayan Hieroglyphic Writing: The "Affix Cluster"', in *Phoneticism in Mayan Hieroglyphic Writing*, John S. Justeson and Lyle Campbell (eds.), pp. 212–233; Schele, Linda, 1990 'The Demotion of Chac Zutz': Lineage Compounds and Subsidiary Lords at Palenque', in Greene Robertson; Stuart, David S. and Stephen Houston, 1990, 'A Title of Subordinates at Classic Maya Courts', manuscript on file with the Instituto Hondureño de Antropología e Historia.

12 Recently, David Webster has directed the investigation of the Type 4 site Group 8N-11 in the Sepulturas area, and encountered sculpture which Barbara Fash believes to be war-related. The publication of this material should serve to shed light on the role and status of warriors in the Copán Valley.

Chapter 7 (pp. 139–151)

1 Riese, Berthold, 1986, 'Late Classic Relationship between Copán and Quiriguá: Some Epigraphic Evidence', in *The Southeast Maya Periphery*, Patricia Urban and Edward Schortman (eds.).

2 Gordon 1902.

3 Morley 1920:261.

4 This project was funded by the National Science Foundation, the National Endowment for the Humanities, the National Geographic Society, the Wenner-Gren Foundation for Anthropological Research, the Center for Field Research, Northern Illinois University, and the IHAH. For a summary of the results of the first two seasons of research see Fash 1988.

5 In this we follow the standards and the precedent of the projects conducted by the Oriental Institute of the University of Chicago in Egypt.

6 Proskouriakoff, Tatiana, 1973, pp. 165–178.

7 Pasztory, Esther, 1974, 'The Iconography of the Teotihuacan Tlaloc', *Studies in Precolumbian Art and Archaeology*, No. 15.

8 Personal communications, 1987.

9 Censers of this type have been found throughout the Copán Valley, indicating that the practice of burning incense was common among all social classes. The amount of bloodletting that took place is a hotly-debated question.

10 Sharer, Robert J., 1990.

11 Marcus (1976:138) was the first to note that this often-cited date proclaimed the independence day of Quiriguá.

12 Sharer, Robert J., 1978, 'Archaeology and History at Quiriguá', *Journal of Field Archaeology* 5:51–70.

13 Ashmore, Wendy, 1984, 'Quiriguá Archaeology and History Revisited', *Journal of Field Archaeology* 111:365–380.

Chapter 8 (pp. 153–172)

1 See Schele and Freidel, *A Forest of Kings* (Chapter 8); earlier glosses for his name include 'Yax "Sun-at-Horizon"'; 'New Horizon"'; 'Dawn' ('Madrugada' in Spanish); 'New Dawn'; and 'Rising Sun'.

2 As first demonstrated in the survey and excavations undertaken by Gordon Willey; Willey, Leventhal, and Fash 1978; Willey and Leventhal 1979.

3 Fash, William L. and Kurt Z. Long, 1983, 'Mapa Arqueologico del Valle de Copan', in Baudez Vol. 3; Fash, William L., 1983c, 'Introduccion al Mapa', in Baudez Vol. 3.

4 Kurjack, Edward B., 1974, *Prehistoric Lowland Maya Community and Social Organization: A Case Study at Dzibilchaltun, Yucatán, Mexico*.

5 Sanders 1986:13.

6 Ashmore, Wendy, 1989, 'El Proyecto Arqueológico Copán de Cosmología: Conceptos de direccionalidad entre los antiguos Mayas', paper presented at the V Seminario de Arqueología Hondureña, Copán Ruinas, Copán.

7 Wisdom, Charles, 1940, *The Chorti Indians of Guatemala* (reprint, 1974).

8 Leventhal, Richard M., 1981, 'Settlement Patterns in the Southeast Maya Area', in Wendy Ashmore (ed.), pp. 187–209.

9 Turner *et al* 1983.

10 Leventhal 1981.

11 Wirth, Louis, 1938, 'Urbanism as a Way of Life', in *American Journal of Sociology* 44:3–24.

12 Personal communications with Arthur Demarest, 1986.

13 Fash 1983b:468.

14 Willey, Leventhal, and Fash 1978.

15 Schele, Linda, 1989, 'Altar F' and Structure 32', in *Copán Notes*, Number 46.

16 Morley 1920:381.

17 Nakamura, Seiichi, 1987, 'Reconocimiento Arqueologico en los Valles', *Yaxkin*, Vol. 10 (1):1–38.

18 Marcus 1976:148.

Chapter 9 (pp. 173–183)

1 Shimkin, Demitri B., 1973, 'Models for the Downfall: Some Ecological and Culture-Historical Considerations', in *The Classic Maya Collapse*, T. Patrick Culbert (ed.), p. 291.

2 Culbert 1973.

3 Shimkin 1973.

4 Fash 1983d:304.

5 Webster, David and AnnCorinne Freter, 1989, 'Settlement History and the Classic Collapse at Copan: A Redefined Chronological Perspective', *Latin American Antiquity* 1:66–85.

6 Thompson, J. Eric S., 1971, *The Rise and Fall of Classic Maya Civilization*.

7 Landa, Diego de, in Tozzer 1941:37.

8 Paine, Richard, 1990, 'The Dynamics of Collapse:

Household Abandonment at Copán', paper presented at the 89th Annual Meeting of the American Anthropological Association.

9 Baudez 1983 (Vol. 2):497.

10 Webster, David (ed.), 1989, pp. 32–33.

11 Sanders, William T., 'Ecological Succession in the Copán Valley', manuscript on file with the Instituto Hondureño de Antropología e Historia.

12 Turner II, B.L. *et al*, 1983, 'Habitat y Agricultura en la Region de Copan', in Baudez.

13 Fash 1983d:306–308.

14 Abrams, Elliot and David Rue, 1989, 'The Causes and Consequences of Deforestation among the Prehistoric Maya', *Human Ecology* 16:377–395.

15 This is one of the sad 'universals' in human culture history.

16 Storey, Rebecca, 1987, 'Mortalidad Durante el

Classico Tardio en Copán y el Cajón', paper presented at the IV Seminario de Arqueología Hondureña, La Ceiba, Honduras.

17 Willey, Gordon R., and Demitri B. Shimkin, 1973, 'The Maya Collapse: A Summary View', in Culbert, pp. 457–502.

18 Tambiah, Stanley, 1977, 'The Galactic Polity: The Structure of Traditional Kingdoms in Southeast Asia', *Annals of New York Academy of Sciences* 293:69–97.

19 Marcus, Joyce, 'Ancient Maya Political Organization', paper presented at the 1989 Dumbarton Oaks Conference.

20 This dynamic model has the additional advantage of being based on the ethnohistorical and archaeological data on the Maya themselves, a consideration long recommended by the pre-eminent Mayanist Robert Sharer. Morley and Brainerd, 1991, *The Ancient Maya*.

Acknowledgments

Any attempt to synthesize the work at Copán owes much to the efforts of many people. Sadly, it is possible to name only a few of them here. Gordon R. Willey's Copán Valley Project was the origin of the modern era of Copán archaeology and his inspiration and support are greatly appreciated. The directors of the two phases of the subsequent Honduran Government-sponsored Copán Archaeological Project, Claude F. Baudez (Phase I) and William T. Sanders (Phase II), were also strongly supportive. Phase I (1977–1980) was financed by the Central American Bank and Phase II (1980–1985) by the World Bank, with supplementary funding obtained by Sanders and his Co-Director David Webster from the National Science Foundation and other sources.

The Honduran Institute of Anthropology and History (IHAH) has firmly backed all the modern Copán projects. Special thanks are due to the Director of the Institute, José Maria Casco, and to his predecessors Victor Cruz Reyes, Ricardo Agurcia Fasquelle, Vito Veliz Ramirez, and José Adán Cueva. Particularly important has been the advice of Ricardo Agurcia Fasquelle, and the invaluable goodwill of Oscar Cruz Melgar (Regional Representative of the IHAH in Copán) over the past 15 years. All but a handful of the illustrations in this book, and most of the research results presented here, appear courtesy of the IHAH. Likewise, the author is grateful to President Rafael Leonardo Callejas for his personal interest in the work at Copán. The people of the town of Copán Ruinas have been our gracious hosts, good friends and in many cases co-workers for many years.

The Copán Mosaics Project (1985–present), the Hieroglyphic Stairway Project (1986–1989), and the Copán Acropolis Archaeological Project (1988–present) have been financed (in chronological order of initial funding) by the Center for Field Research, Northern Illinois University, the National Geographic Society, the National Science Foundation, the National Endowment for the Humanities, the Wenner-Gren Foundation for Anthropological Research, the H.J. Heinz III Charitable Fund, the Council for International Exchange of Scholars (Fulbright Program), the IHAH, the U.S. Agency for International Development, the University of Texas, the University of Pennsylvania, Tulane University, and the Asociacion de Estudios Precolombinos Copán through the Honduran Fund for Social Investment (FHIS). Special recognition should be given to the National Geographic Society for its long-term interest and funding, and in particular to George Stuart, Senior Assistant Editor of NGS, for his advocacy, advice, and the remarkable discovery and donation to the IHAH of the Raul Pavon Abreu archive.

Many colleagues on the research projects directed by the author have been essential to the success of the overall enterprise, above all, Carlos Rudy Larios Villalta, the Project Co-Director in charge of restoration, and Barbara W. Fash, our Chief Artist and Sculpture Coordinator.

The scope of the Copán Acropolis Archaeological Project has been made possible through the outstanding contributions of the three other Co-Directors: Robert J. Sharer (directing the East Court investigations); Ricardo

Agurcia Fasquelle (directing the Structure 10L-16 investigations); and E. Wyllys Andrews V (directing the Group 10L-2 investigations).

Of fundamental importance to the research has been the decipherment of the hieroglyphic inscriptions carried out (in chronological order of joining) by Linda Schele, David Stuart, Nikolai Grube, and Floyd Lounsbury, with valuable insights also provided by Peter Mathews and Stephen Houston. Schele and Stuart have also drawn a number of the inscriptions under study, and provided invaluable historical insights for the interpretation of the archaeological remains. Study of the pictorial sculpture has been conducted by Barbara Fash, Linda Schele, Jeff Karl Kowalski, and David Stuart.

Other staff members include David Sedat, Alfonso Morales, Jean-Pierre Courau, Juan Ramon Guerra, Fernando Lopez, Reyna Flores, and – in earlier phases of the Copán research – Richard Leventhal, B.L. Turner II, William Johnson, Gail Mahood, Rene Viel, Berthold Riese, Elliot Abrams, David Rue, AnnCorinne Freter, and Wendy Ashmore. David Grove deserves much gratitude for bringing Thames and Hudson and the author together on this book project. Many thanks are also due to my students and to William L. Fash (Sr.) and Ruth E. Fash; Ron and Leah Fash; Charles Roska; Elena Fash; Don and Pat Wascher; Ron and Jacques Mazanowski; Cecil and Pamela Brown; James and Nancy

Norris; Ian Graham; Maria Amalia de Agurcia, Bertha Lydia de Cruz; Carla Castaneda; J. Raul and Maria de Welchez; and Cristiana Nufio de Figueroa. Special thanks go to George and Martha Molanphy for the use of their telephone and fax machine and the sharing of their vehicles, expertise, hospitality and friendship over the years.

Other sources of illustrations

All photographs are by the author except for the following, which are by courtesy of:
Jean Pierre Courau VII, 9, 10, 11–14, 25, 26, 49, 51, 67, 70, 78, 81, 107
Barbara Fash I, 21, 82, 83, 86
Reyna Flores 53–57, 92, 93
Edward Kurjack 29
National Geographic Society X (photo Kenneth Garrett), 89 (painting by Tom Hall)
Peabody Museum, Harvard University 7 (photo Hillel Burger), 16 (photo Hillel Burger), 22, 23, 88
University of Oklahoma Press 3

All drawings are by Barbara Fash except for the following:
José Humberto Espinoza 33, 47
Barbara Fash and Refugio Murcia 8, 95
Rudy Larios 48, 52 (assisted by Jorge Ramos, Barbara Fash and José Humberto Espinoza)

Index

Numerals in *italics* refer to illustration numbers. d = deity; r = ruler; loc = location; w = ward of Copán